asian

asian

MURDOCH BOOKS

contents

asian noodles

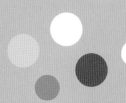

Asian food is varied and intriguing, with noodles a popular feature. Appearing in many different guises (fresh or dried, broad or threadlike, simmered or fried, hot or cold, made of wheat, rice flour, mung bean or even buckwheat), the world of the noodle is an alluring one indeed. Despite the romantic theories involving Marco Polo taking noodles back to Europe to teach the Italians a thing or two, Asian noodles and Italian pastas actually developed, so historians say, quite independently of each other. The world's oldest noodle remains were found in China a few years ago and were reckoned to be 4000 years old, making the noodle a truly ancient and venerable food.

In its myriad forms, noodles are a staple all over Asia. They're consumed for breakfast, lunch and dinner plus all snack times in between. In fact, the noodle is more than mere food; the Chinese, for example, believe that eating noodles will lengthen your life and some communities serve it at birthday parties, instead of a cake! But whatever the history, lore and legends surrounding noodles, the bottom line can't be denied — namely, that noodles are delicious. Who can resist a plate of pad Thai, rich with prawn (or chicken), egg and peanuts and tasting of a smoky wok? Or laksa, that clever Malay marriage of rice noodles and lush, spicy, coconut-milk soup that's surely one of the most satisfying combinations of all time? Noodles are versatile and can be fashioned into everything from hurled-together meals suited to relaxed family dining, to far more elegant preparations, worthy of a king.

start

Crispy Asian noodle pancakes

150 g (5½ oz) dried rice vermicelli
3 tablespoons chopped coriander (cilantro) leaves
3 spring onions (scallions), thinly sliced
1 small red chilli, finely chopped
1 lemongrass stem, white part only, finely chopped
1 garlic clove, crushed
oil, for shallow-frying

Soak the vermicelli in boiling water for 5–7 minutes, or until soft. Rinse under cold water, drain, then dry with paper towels.

Place the noodles in a bowl with the coriander, spring onion, chilli, lemongrass and garlic. Season to taste with salt and mix together.

Heat the oil in a heavy-based frying pan and shallow-fry 2 tablespoons of the mixture in hot oil. Flatten with a spatula while cooking and fry until crisp and golden on both sides. Drain on crumpled paper towels and sprinkle with salt. Repeat with the rest of the noodle mixture.

MAKES ABOUT 25

Fresh vegetarian rice paper rolls

Dipping sauce
3 tablespoons sweet chilli sauce
1 tablespoon lime juice

100 g (3½ oz) dried rice
vermicelli
½ green mango, julienned
1 small Lebanese (short)
cucumber, seeded and
julienned
½ avocado, julienned

4 spring onions (scallions),
thinly sliced
1 large handful coriander
(cilantro) leaves
2 tablespoons chopped
Vietnamese mint
1 tablespoon sweet chilli sauce
2 tablespoons lime juice
20 x 15 cm (6 inch) square rice
paper wrappers

To make the dipping sauce, mix together the chilli sauce and lime juice.

Soak the vermicelli in boiling water for 5–7 minutes, or until soft. Drain, then cut into short lengths with scissors.

Put the vermicelli, mango, cucumber, avocado, spring onion, coriander, mint, sweet chilli sauce and lime juice in a bowl and mix together well.

Working with no more than two rice paper wrappers at a time, dip each wrapper in a bowl of warm water for 10 seconds to soften, then lay out on a flat work surface. Put 1 tablespoon of the filling on the wrapper, fold in the sides and roll up tightly. Repeat with the remaining filling and rice paper wrappers. Serve immediately with the dipping sauce.

MAKES 20

Mini Thai spring rolls

Filling
80 g (2¾ oz) dried rice vermicelli
2 garlic cloves, crushed
1 carrot, grated
4 spring onions (scallions), finely chopped
1 tablespoon sweet chilli sauce
2 teaspoons grated fresh ginger
2 coriander (cilantro) roots, finely chopped
1½ tablespoons lime juice
1 teaspoon grated palm sugar (jaggery) or soft brown sugar
2 tablespoons chopped coriander (cilantro) leaves
3 teaspoons sesame oil
1 tablespoon kecap manis

40 x 12.5 cm (5 inch) square spring roll wrappers
oil, for deep-frying
sweet chilli sauce, to serve

Soak the vermicelli in boiling water for 5–7 minutes, or until soft. Drain, then cut into short lengths with scissors. Mix with the remaining filling ingredients.

Working with one wrapper at a time, spoon 1 tablespoon of the filling onto one corner, brush the edges with water and roll up on the diagonal, tucking in the edges as you go. Repeat with the remaining filling and wrappers.

Fill a wok or deep heavy-based saucepan one-third full of oil and heat to 180°C (350°F), or until a cube of bread browns in 15 seconds. Cook in batches for 2 minutes, or until golden. Drain on crumpled paper towels. Serve with sweet chilli sauce.

MAKES 40

Udon noodle sushi rolls

300 g (10½ oz) dried flat udon or soba (buckwheat) noodles
6 nori sheets
50 g (1¾ oz) pickled daikon, cut into long, thin strips
3 tablespoons drained red pickled ginger shreds
ponzu sauce, for dipping (see Note)

Cook the noodles in a large saucepan of boiling water for 5 minutes, or until tender. Drain, rinse under cold water, then pat dry.

Working on a flat work surface, lay out one sheet of nori on a sushi mat. Neatly lay one-sixth of the noodles along the bottom half of the nori, then arrange the daikon and pickled ginger along the centre of the noodles. Roll the nori up firmly to enclose the filling. Cut the roll in half and then each half into three equal pieces. Repeat with the remaining ingredients. Serve with ponzu sauce.

MAKES 36 PIECES

NOTE: Ponzu is a popular Japanese dipping sauce made from rice vinegar, soy, mirin and dashi.

Pork and noodle balls

Dipping sauce
125 ml (4 fl oz/½ cup) Japanese
   soy sauce
4 tablespoons sweet chilli sauce
2 teaspoons mirin
2 teaspoons finely chopped
   fresh ginger

250 g (9 oz) hokkien (egg)
   noodles
2 garlic cloves, crushed

300 g (10½ oz) minced
   (ground) pork
6 spring onions (scallions),
   finely chopped
4 tablespoons finely chopped
   coriander (cilantro) leaves
1 tablespoon fish sauce
2 tablespoons oyster sauce
1½ tablespoons lime juice
oil, for deep-frying

To make the dipping sauce, combine the ingredients in a bowl.

Soak the noodles in boiling water for 1 minute, or until tender and separated. Drain well and pat dry with paper towels. Cut the noodles into 5 cm (2 inch) lengths with scissors, then transfer to a large bowl. Add the garlic, pork, spring onion, coriander leaves, fish sauce, oyster sauce and lime juice and mix well using your hands, making sure the pork is evenly distributed throughout the noodles.

Roll a tablespoon of mixture at a time into a ball to make 30 in total, pressing each ball firmly to ensure they stick together during cooking.

Fill a wok or deep heavy-based saucepan one-third full of oil and heat to 170°C (325°F), or until a cube of bread browns in 20 seconds. Deep-fry the pork balls in batches for 2–3 minutes, or until golden and cooked through. Drain on crumpled paper towels. Serve hot with the dipping sauce.

MAKES 30

Prawn and baby corn rice noodle rolls

1 tablespoon peanut oil
2 garlic cloves, crushed
200 g (7 oz) fresh shiitake
    mushrooms, thinly sliced
5 spring onions (scallions),
    chopped
4 tablespoons drained and
    chopped water chestnuts
650 g (1 lb 7 oz) raw medium
    prawns (shrimp), peeled,
    deveined and chopped

150 g (5½ oz) fresh baby corn,
    roughly chopped
500 g (1 lb 2 oz) fresh rice noodle
    roll, at room temperature
oil, for brushing

Dipping sauce

3 tablespoons light soy sauce
2 teaspoons sesame oil
1 teaspoon grated fresh ginger
1 teaspoon sugar
2 tablespoons Chinese rice wine

Heat a wok over high heat, add the peanut oil and swirl to coat. Add the garlic and mushrooms and stir-fry for 1 minute, or until soft. Add the spring onion, water chestnuts, prawns and baby corn and cook for 2 minutes. Remove from the heat.

Unroll one noodle roll and cut it in half. You need two 16 x 24 cm (6¼ x 9½ inch) rectangles. Place 3 tablespoons of the prawn mixture along one short end of each rectangle, leaving a 3 cm (1¼ inch) border. Fold both sides of the noodle roll towards the centre, then roll up like a spring roll. Cover with a damp cloth and repeat.

Line a bamboo steamer with baking paper, brush with a little oil, then place the rolls in, seam side down. Place the steamer over a wok filled with simmering water, cover and steam for 4–5 minutes, or until the prawns are cooked through.

Gently warm the dipping sauce ingredients in a saucepan, then drizzle over the rolls.

SERVES 4

Noodle tempura with wasabi dressing

Wasabi dressing
1/2 teaspoon wasabi paste
1 1/2 tablespoons Japanese soy
    sauce
3 tablespoons mirin

80 g (2¾ oz) dried ramen
    noodles

1 carrot, grated
2 nori sheets, thinly sliced
2 spring onions (scallions),
    thinly sliced
155 g (5½ oz/1¼ cups) tempura
    flour
250 ml (9 fl oz/1 cup) iced water
oil, for deep-frying

Mix the wasabi paste and a little of the soy sauce to make a smooth paste.
Add the mirin and remaining soy sauce and stir until there are no lumps.

Cook the noodles in a large saucepan of boiling water for 5 minutes, or until
tender. Drain, then rinse under cold water. Cut into 5 cm (2 inch) lengths with
scissors. Transfer to a bowl. Mix in the carrot, nori and spring onion. Chill.

Place the tempura flour in a large bowl and make a well in the centre. Pour in the
iced water and stir gently with chopsticks or a fork, until the flour and water are
just combined (the batter should still be a little lumpy).

Fill a wok or deep heavy-based saucepan one-third full of oil and heat to 180°C
(350°F), or until a cube of bread browns in 15 seconds. Combine the noodle
mixture and tempura batter, tossing lightly. Spoon 3 tablespoons of the mixture
into the oil and, using a fork or chopsticks, quickly and carefully spread the
mixture out a little. Cook for about 3 minutes, turning occasionally, or until
golden and cooked through. Remove and drain. Keep warm in a low oven while
you repeat with the remaining mixture. Serve with the wasabi dressing.

SERVES 4

Prawn, snow pea and coriander rice noodle rolls

Dipping sauce
2 tablespoons light soy sauce
3 tablespoons rice vinegar

3 dried shiitake mushrooms
350 g (12 oz) raw prawns
(shrimp), peeled and deveined
2 garlic cloves, crushed
4 spring onions (scallions),
chopped
60 g (2¼ oz) snow peas
(mangetout), chopped

2 teaspoons finely chopped
fresh ginger
1 large handful coriander
(cilantro) leaves, chopped
100 g (3½ oz) water chestnuts,
chopped
1 teaspoon sesame oil
1 tablespoon light soy sauce
1 egg white
1 teaspoon cornflour (cornstarch)
300 g (10½ oz) fresh rice noodle
roll, at room temperature

To make the dipping sauce, combine the soy sauce and rice vinegar.

Soak the mushrooms in boiling water for 20 minutes. Drain. Discard the stems and finely chop the caps.

Mince the prawns in a food processor. Mix in the mushrooms, garlic, spring onion, snow peas, ginger, coriander, water chestnuts, sesame oil, soy sauce and a pinch of salt. Add the egg white and cornflour and pulse until smooth. Unroll the noodle roll and cut into six 15 cm (6 inch) squares. Spread 3 tablespoons of filling evenly over each square and roll firmly to form a log.

Line a large bamboo steamer with baking paper, brush with a little oil, then place the rolls in, seam side down. Place the steamer over a wok filled with simmering water, cover and steam for 5 minutes. Cut each roll in half and serve with the sauce.

MAKES 12

Pork and prawn spring rolls

50 g (1¾ oz) cellophane noodles (mung bean vermicelli)
1 tablespoon oil
2 large garlic cloves, crushed
2 tablespoons grated fresh ginger
6 spring onions (scallions), chopped
4 coriander (cilantro) roots, finely chopped
200 g (7 oz) peeled raw prawns (shrimp), minced

200 g (7 oz) minced (ground) pork
1 carrot, grated
3 tablespoons finely chopped coriander (cilantro) leaves
2 tablespoons sweet chilli sauce
1 tablespoon fish sauce
2 tablespoons soy sauce
30 small spring roll wrappers
1 egg white, lightly beaten
oil, extra, for deep-frying

Soak the noodles in boiling water for 3–4 minutes, or until soft. Drain, then rinse under cold water. Cut them into short lengths with scissors.

Heat the oil in a large saucepan over medium heat. Add the garlic, ginger, spring onion and coriander root. Cook for 1–2 minutes, then add the prawn and pork and stir until cooked through. Stir in the noodles, carrot and coriander leaves. Cook for 1 minute. Add the sweet chilli, fish and soy sauces and cook until dry. Cool.

Place a tablespoon of the mixture along the centre of each wrapper. Brush the edge with egg white and roll up, tucking in the ends as you go. Cover to prevent drying.

Fill a wok or deep heavy-based saucepan one-third full of oil and heat to 190°C (375°F), or until a cube of bread browns in 10 seconds. Cook the rolls in batches for 30–60 seconds, or until golden. Drain on crumpled paper towels.

MAKES 30

Prawn, noodle and nori parcels

Dipping sauce
4 tablespoons tonkatsu sauce or barbecue sauce
2 tablespoons lemon juice
1 tablespoon sake or mirin
1–2 teaspoons grated fresh ginger

250 g (9 oz) dried somen noodles
3 nori sheets
60 g (2¼ oz/½ cup) plain (all-purpose) flour
2 egg yolks
24 raw medium prawns (shrimp), peeled and deveined, tails intact
oil, for deep-frying

Combine the dipping sauce ingredients, adding the ginger to taste.

Using a sharp knife, cut the noodles to the same length as the prawns (from the head to the base of the tail). Keep the noodles in neat bundles. Cut the nori into 2.5 cm (1 inch) wide strips.

Sift the flour into a bowl and make a well in the centre. Mix the egg yolks with 3 tablespoons of water. Gradually add to the flour, whisking to make a smooth batter. Add another tablespoon of water if the mixture is too thick.

Dip a prawn in the batter, letting the excess run off. Roll the prawn lengthways in noodles to coat it with a single layer. Keep the noodles in place by rolling a nori strip around the centre of the prawn and securing it with a little batter. Repeat.

Fill a wok or deep heavy-based saucepan one-third full of oil and heat to 180°C (350°F), or until a cube of bread browns in 15 seconds. Deep-fry 2–3 prawns at a time for 1–2 minutes. Drain on crumpled paper towels. Serve with the dipping sauce.

MAKES 24

Vietnamese rice paper rolls

Dipping sauce
185 ml (6 fl oz/¾ cup) fish sauce
3 tablespoons lime juice
2 tablespoons grated palm sugar
(jaggery) or soft brown sugar
2 bird's eye chillies, seeded and
finely chopped

150 g (5½ oz) dried rice
vermicelli

48 round 15 cm (6 inch) rice
paper wrappers
48 cooked king prawns
(shrimp), peeled, deveined
and halved lengthways
150 g (5½ oz) bean sprouts
60 g (2¼ oz/3 cups) mint
60 g (2¼ oz/2 cups) coriander
(cilantro) leaves

To make the dipping sauce, combine all the ingredients and 125 ml (4 fl oz/½ cup) water in a bowl and stir until the sugar dissolves. Transfer to two small serving dishes and set aside.

Soak the vermicelli in boiling water for 5–7 minutes, or until soft. Drain.

Assemble the rolls one at a time. Dip a rice paper wrapper in a bowl of warm water for 30 seconds, or until it softens. Place the wrapper on a work surface and put 2 prawn halves on the bottom third of the wrapper. Top with a few noodles, bean sprouts, 3 mint leaves and 6 coriander leaves, in that order. Ensure that the filling is neat and compact, then turn up the bottom of the wrapper to cover the filling. Holding the filling in place, fold in the two sides, then roll up.

Arrange on a platter, seam side down. Cover with a damp cloth or plastic wrap until ready to serve. Serve with the dipping sauce.

MAKES 48

Deep-fried chicken and noodle balls

50 g (1¾ oz) dried rice vermicelli
500 g (1 lb 2 oz) minced (ground) chicken
3 garlic cloves, finely chopped
1 tablespoon chopped fresh ginger
1 red chilli, seeded and finely chopped
2 spring onions (scallions), thinly sliced
4 tablespoons chopped coriander (cilantro) leaves
1 egg, lightly beaten
4 tablespoons plain (all-purpose) flour
4 tablespoons finely chopped water chestnuts
oil, for deep-frying

Dipping sauce
125 ml (4 fl oz/½ cup) sweet chilli sauce
125 ml (4 fl oz/½ cup) soy sauce
1 tablespoon Chinese rice wine

Soak the vermicelli in boiling water for 5–7 minutes, or until soft. Drain, then cut into short lengths with scissors.

Combine the chicken, garlic, ginger, chilli, spring onion, coriander, egg, flour and water chestnuts in a large bowl. Mix in the vermicelli and season with salt. Refrigerate for 30 minutes. Roll heaped tablespoons of mixture into balls.

To make the dipping sauce, mix the sweet chilli sauce, soy sauce and rice wine.

Fill a wok or deep heavy-based saucepan one-third full with oil and heat to 180°C (350°F), or until a cube of bread browns in 15 seconds. Deep-fry the balls in batches for 2 minutes, or until golden brown and cooked through. Drain on crumpled paper towels and serve with the dipping sauce.

MAKES ABOUT 30

Duck rice noodle rolls

700 g (1 lb 9 oz) barbecued or roast duck
8 fresh rice noodle rolls, at room temperature
2 spring onions (scallions), thinly sliced
2 thick slices fresh ginger, thinly sliced
1 handful coriander (cilantro) leaves
oyster sauce, for drizzling
chilli sauce, to serve

Cut the duck into bite-sized pieces. You may have to strip the flesh off the bones first, depending on how you bought it — leave the skin on but trim off any fatty bits.

Carefully unroll the rice noodle rolls. Put a pile of duck (an eighth of the whole amount) at one edge of the narrower end of one noodle roll and arrange some spring onion, ginger and coriander over it. Drizzle with about a teaspoon of oyster sauce and roll the sheet up. Repeat this with the remaining sheets. Put the sheets on a heatproof plate.

Put the plate in a bamboo or metal steamer and set the steamer above a wok filled with simmering water. Cover and steam for 5 minutes.

Serve the rolls cut into lengths with some more oyster sauce drizzled over them and some chilli sauce on the side.

SERVES 4

slurp

Miso soup with chicken and udon noodles

8 dried shiitake mushrooms
600 g (1 lb 5 oz) boneless, skinless chicken breasts, cut into 1.5 cm (⅝ inch) thick strips
3 tablespoons white miso paste
2 teaspoons dashi granules
1 tablespoon wakame flakes or other seaweed (see Note)

300 g (10½ oz) baby bok choy (pak choy), halved lengthways
400 g (14 oz) fresh udon noodles
150 g (5½ oz) silken firm tofu, cut into 1 cm (½ inch) cubes
3 spring onions (scallions), sliced on the diagonal

Soak the mushrooms in 250 ml (9 fl oz/1 cup) boiling water for 20 minutes. Drain, reserving the liquid. Discard the stalks and thinly slice the caps.

Pour 2 litres (70 fl oz/8 cups) water into a saucepan and bring to the boil, then reduce the heat and simmer. Add the chicken and cook for 2–3 minutes, or until almost cooked through.

Add the mushrooms and cook for 1 minute, then add the miso paste, dashi granules, wakame and reserved mushroom liquid. Stir to dissolve the dashi and miso paste. Do not allow it to boil.

Add the bok choy halves and simmer for 1 minute, or until beginning to wilt, then add the noodles and simmer for a further 2 minutes. Gently stir in the tofu and ladle the hot soup into large serving bowls. Garnish with the sliced spring onion.

SERVES 4–6

NOTE: Wakame is a curly-leafed, brown algae with a mild vegetable taste and a soft texture. It can be used in salads or can be boiled and served like a vegetable. Use a small amount as it swells by about ten times after being cooked.

Sukiyaki

Sauce
½–1 teaspoon dashi granules
4 tablespoons soy sauce
2 tablespoons sake
2 tablespoons mirin
1 tablespoon caster (superfine)
    sugar

300 g (10½ oz) shirataki
    noodles (see Note)
50 g (1¾ oz) lard

5 large spring onions (scallions),
    cut into 1 cm (½ inch) slices
    on the diagonal
16 fresh shiitake mushrooms,
    chopped if too large
800 g (1 lb 12 oz) rump steak,
    thinly sliced across the grain
    (first freeze for 40 minutes)
100 g (3½ oz) watercress,
    trimmed
4 eggs (optional)

To make the sauce, dissolve the dashi granules in 125 ml (4 fl oz/½ cup) water in a bowl. Stir in the soy sauce, sake, mirin and caster sugar.

Drain the noodles, place in a large heatproof bowl, cover with boiling water and soak for 2 minutes. Rinse under cold water and drain well.

Melt the lard in a large frying pan over medium heat. Cook the spring onion, mushrooms and beef in batches, stirring continuously, for 1–2 minutes each batch, or until just brown. Return all the meat, spring onion and mushrooms to the pan, then add the sauce and watercress. Cook for 1 minute, or until the watercress has wilted — the sauce should just cover the ingredients.

To serve, divide the noodles among four serving bowls and spoon the sauce evenly over the top. If desired, crack an egg into each bowl and break up through the soup using chopsticks until it partially cooks.

SERVES 4

NOTE: Shirataki noodles are sold in the refrigerated section of Japanese supermarkets.

Scallops with soba noodles and dashi broth

250 g (9 oz) dried soba
  (buckwheat) noodles
3 tablespoons mirin
3 tablespoons soy sauce
2 teaspoons rice vinegar
1 teaspoon dashi granules
2 spring onions (scallions), sliced
  on the diagonal

1 teaspoon finely chopped
  fresh ginger
24 large scallops, without roe,
  membrane removed
5 fresh black fungus, chopped
  (see Note)
1 nori sheet, shredded,
  to garnish

Cook the noodles in a large saucepan of boiling water for 5 minutes, or until tender. Drain, then rinse under cold water.

Place the mirin, soy sauce, rice vinegar, dashi granules and 750 ml (26 fl oz/3 cups) water in a saucepan. Bring to the boil, then reduce the heat and simmer for about 4 minutes. Add the spring onion and ginger to the pan and keep at a gentle simmer until needed.

Heat a chargrill pan or barbecue hotplate until very hot and sear the scallops on both sides, in batches, for 1 minute.

Divide the noodles and black fungus among four deep serving bowls. Pour 185 ml (6 fl oz/3⁄4 cup) broth into each bowl and top with 6 scallops each. Garnish with the nori and serve immediately.

SERVES 4

NOTE: If you can't buy fresh black fungus, use dried instead but soak it in warm water for 15–20 minutes before use.

Roast pork, Chinese cabbage and noodle hotpot

70 g (2½ oz) cellophane noodles (mung bean vermicelli)
250 g (9 oz) Chinese cabbage (wong bok)
1 litre (35 fl oz/4 cups) chicken stock
2.5 x 2.5 cm (1 x 1 inch) piece fresh ginger, thinly sliced
350 g (12 oz) Chinese barbecued pork (char siu)
2 spring onions (scallions), thinly sliced on the diagonal
2 tablespoons light soy sauce
1 tablespoon Chinese rice wine
½ teaspoon sesame oil

Soak the noodles in boiling water for 3–4 minutes, or until soft. Drain, then rinse under cold water.

Separate the cabbage leaves and cut the leafy ends from the stems. Cut both the cabbage stems and leaves into 2–3 cm (¾–1¼ inch) squares.

Pour the stock into a 2 litre (70 fl oz/8 cup) flameproof hotpot or casserole dish, add the ginger slices and bring to the boil over high heat. Add the cabbage stems and cook for 2 minutes, then add the cabbage leaves and cook for a further 1 minute. Reduce the heat to medium, add the noodles and cook, covered, for 4–5 minutes, stirring occasionally.

Meanwhile, cut the pork into 2 cm (¾ inch) cubes and add to the noodles, along with the spring onion, soy sauce, rice wine and sesame oil. Stir to combine, then cook, covered, for 3–4 minutes before serving.

SERVES 4

Five-spice duck and somen noodle soup

4 duck breasts, skin on
1 teaspoon Chinese five-spice
1 teaspoon oil
200 g (7 oz) dried somen noodles

Star anise broth
1 litre (35 fl oz/4 cups) chicken stock
3 whole star anise
5 spring onions (scallions), chopped
3 tablespoons chopped coriander (cilantro) leaves

Preheat the oven to 200°C (400°F/Gas 6). Trim the duck breast of excess fat, then lightly sprinkle both sides with the five-spice.

Heat the oil in a large frying pan. Add the duck, skin side down, and cook over medium heat for 2–3 minutes, or until brown and crisp. Turn and cook the other side for 3 minutes. Transfer to a baking tray and cook, skin side up, for another 8–10 minutes, or until cooked to your liking.

Meanwhile, place the chicken stock and star anise in a small saucepan. Bring to the boil, then reduce the heat and simmer for 5 minutes. Add the spring onion and coriander and simmer for 5 minutes.

Cook the noodles in a large saucepan of boiling water for 2 minutes, or until tender. Drain, then rinse under cold water. Divide among four bowls. Ladle the broth over the noodles and top each bowl with one sliced duck breast.

SERVES 4

Prawn laksa

1½ tablespoons ground
   coriander
1 tablespoon ground cumin
1 teaspoon ground turmeric
1 onion, roughly chopped
1 x 3 cm (½ x 1¼ inch) piece
   fresh ginger, roughly chopped
3 garlic cloves
3 lemongrass stems, white part
   only, sliced
6 macadamia nuts
4–6 small red chillies
2–3 teaspoons shrimp paste
1 litre (35 fl oz/4 cups) chicken
   stock
3 tablespoons oil

4 makrut (kaffir lime) leaves
2½ tablespoons lime juice
2 tablespoons fish sauce
750 ml (26 fl oz/3 cups) coconut
   milk
2 tablespoons soft brown sugar
750 g (1 lb 10 oz) raw medium
   prawns (shrimp), peeled and
   deveined, tails intact
250 g (9 oz) dried rice vermicelli
90 g (3¼ oz/1 cup) bean sprouts
4 fried tofu puffs, julienned
3 tablespoons roughly chopped
   Vietnamese mint
2 large handfuls coriander
   (cilantro) leaves

Place all of the spices, onion, ginger, garlic, lemongrass, macadamias, chillies and shrimp paste in a blender, add 125 ml (4 fl oz/½ cup) of stock and blend to a paste. Heat the oil over low heat, add the paste and cook for 3–5 minutes, stirring constantly. Add the remaining stock, bring to the boil, then reduce to a simmer for 15 minutes, or until reduced slightly. Add the lime leaves, lime juice, fish sauce, coconut milk and sugar and simmer for 5 minutes. Add the prawns and cook for 2 minutes, or until they are pink and cooked. Do not boil or cover.

Soak the vermicelli in boiling water for 5–7 minutes, or until soft. Drain, then divide among serving bowls with most of the sprouts. Ladle hot soup over the noodles and top with tofu, mint, coriander leaves and the remaining bean sprouts.

SERVES 4–6

Asian chicken noodle soup

3 dried Chinese mushrooms
185 g (6½ oz) dried thin egg noodles
1 tablespoon oil
4 spring onions (scallions), julienned
1 tablespoon soy sauce
2 tablespoons rice wine, mirin or sherry
1.25 litres (44 fl oz/5 cups) chicken stock
½ small barbecued chicken, shredded
50 g (1¾ oz) sliced ham, cut into strips
90 g (3¼ oz/1 cup) bean sprouts
coriander (cilantro) leaves and thinly
   sliced red chilli, to garnish

Soak the mushrooms in boiling water for 20 minutes. Drain. Discard the stems and thinly slice the caps.

Cook the noodles in a large saucepan of boiling water for 3 minutes, or until tender. Drain. Cut them into short lengths with scissors.

Heat the oil in a large heavy-based saucepan. Add the mushrooms and spring onion. Cook for 1 minute, then add the soy sauce, rice wine and stock. Bring slowly to the boil and cook for 1 minute. Reduce the heat then add the noodles, shredded chicken, ham and bean sprouts. Heat through for 2 minutes without allowing to boil.

Use tongs to divide the noodles among four bowls, ladle in the remaining mixture, and garnish with coriander leaves and sliced chilli.

SERVES 4

Poached seafood broth with soba noodles

250 g (9 oz) dried soba (buckwheat) noodles
8 raw prawns (shrimp)
1½ tablespoons finely chopped fresh ginger
4 spring onions (scallions), sliced on the diagonal
100 ml (3½ fl oz) light soy sauce
3 tablespoons mirin
1 teaspoon grated palm sugar (jaggery) or soft brown sugar

300 g (10½ oz) boneless salmon fillet, skinned and cut into 5 cm (2 inch) thick strips
300 g (10½ oz) boneless white fish fillet, skinned and cut into 5 cm (2 inch) thick strips
150 g (5½ oz) cleaned squid tube, scored and cut into 3 cm (1¼ inch) cubes
50 g (1¾ oz) mizuna, roughly chopped

Cook the noodles in a large saucepan of boiling water for 5 minutes, or until tender. Drain, then rinse under cold water.

Peel and devein the prawns, reserving the shells and leaving the tails intact. Place the heads and shells in a large saucepan with the ginger, half the spring onion and 1.5 litres (52 fl oz/6 cups) water. Bring slowly to the boil and boil for 5 minutes. Strain and discard the prawn heads, shells and spring onion. Return the stock to the pan. Add the soy sauce, mirin and palm sugar to the stock. Heat and stir to dissolve the sugar.

Add the seafood to the pan and poach over low heat for 2–3 minutes, or until it is just cooked. Add the remaining spring onion.

Divide the noodles evenly among four large bowls. Add the seafood, pour on the stock and scatter with the mizuna.

SERVES 4

Chicken laksa

Chicken balls

500 g (1 lb 2 oz) minced (ground) chicken
1 small red chilli, finely chopped
2 garlic cloves, finely chopped
½ small red onion, finely chopped
1 lemongrass stem, white part only, finely chopped
2 tablespoons chopped coriander (cilantro) leaves

200 g (7 oz) dried rice vermicelli
1 tablespoon oil

3 tablespoons good-quality laksa paste
1 litre (35 fl oz/4 cups) chicken stock
500 ml (17 fl oz/2 cups) coconut milk
8 fried tofu puffs, halved on the diagonal
90 g (3¼ oz/1 cup) bean sprouts
2 tablespoons shredded Vietnamese mint
3 tablespoons shredded coriander (cilantro) leaves
lime wedges, to serve
fish sauce, to serve (optional)

To make the chicken balls, process all the ingredients in a food processor until just combined. Roll tablespoons of the mixture into balls with wet hands.

Soak the vermicelli in boiling water for 5–7 minutes, or until soft. Drain well.

Heat the oil in a large saucepan over medium heat. Add the laksa paste and cook for 1–2 minutes, or until aromatic. Add the stock, reduce the heat and simmer for 10 minutes. Add the coconut milk and the chicken balls and simmer for 5 minutes, or until the balls are cooked through.

Divide the vermicelli, tofu puffs and bean sprouts among four serving bowls and ladle the soup over the top, dividing the balls evenly. Garnish with the mint and coriander leaves. Serve with the lime wedges and, if desired, fish sauce.

SERVES 4

Rice noodle soup with duck

1 whole Chinese roast duck
4 coriander (cilantro) roots and
   stems, well rinsed
5 slices fresh galangal
4 spring onions (scallions), sliced
   on the diagonal into 3 cm
   (1¼ inch) lengths
400 g (14 oz) Chinese broccoli
   (gai larn), cut into 5 cm
   (2 inch) lengths

2 garlic cloves, crushed
3 tablespoons fish sauce
1 tablespoon hoisin sauce
2 teaspoons grated palm sugar
   (jaggery) or soft brown sugar
½ teaspoon ground white
   pepper
500 g (1 lb 2 oz) fresh rice
   noodles

To make the stock, cut off the duck's head with a sharp knife and discard. Remove the skin and fat, leaving the neck intact. Carefully remove the flesh from the bones and set aside. Cut any visible fat from the carcass along with the parson's nose, then discard. Break the carcass into large pieces, then place in a large stockpot with 2 litres (70 fl oz/8 cups) water.

Bruise the coriander roots and stems with the back of a knife. Add to the pot with the galangal and bring to the boil. Skim off any foam from the surface. Boil over medium heat for 15 minutes. Strain the stock through a fine sieve, discard the carcass, and return the stock to a clean saucepan.

Slice the duck flesh into strips. Add to the stock with the spring onion, Chinese broccoli, garlic, fish sauce, hoisin sauce, palm sugar and white pepper. Gently bring to the boil.

Cook the noodles in boiling water for 2–3 minutes, or until tender. Drain well. Divide the noodles and soup evenly among the serving bowls.

SERVES 4–6

Teriyaki salmon with soba noodles

12 dried shiitake mushrooms
1 teaspoon dashi granules
3 tablespoons Japanese soy
    sauce
2 tablespoons mirin
½ teaspoon caster (superfine)
    sugar
4 x 150 g (5½ oz) salmon cutlets

3 tablespoons teriyaki marinade
1 tablespoon honey
1 teaspoon sesame oil
250 g (9 oz) dried soba
    (buckwheat) noodles
1 tablespoon peanut oil
2 spring onions (scallions), sliced
    on the diagonal

Soak the mushrooms in 500 ml (17 fl oz/2 cups) boiling water for 10 minutes. Drain, reserving the soaking liquid. Pour the soaking liquid into a saucepan and add the dashi granules, soy sauce, mirin and caster sugar and bring to the boil. Simmer for 5 minutes.

Put the salmon, mushrooms, teriyaki marinade, honey and sesame oil into a non-metallic dish and allow to marinate for 15 minutes.

Cook the noodles in a large saucepan of boiling water for 5 minutes, or until tender. Drain, then rinse under cold water.

Heat the peanut oil in a preheated chargrill pan. Take the salmon and mushrooms out of the marinade and cook over high heat for 3 minutes on each side, or until cooked but still slightly rare in the centre. Pour the marinade over the fish during cooking.

To serve, divide the noodles among four serving bowls, pour over the broth from the mushrooms, then top with the salmon and mushrooms and sprinkle with the spring onion slices.

SERVES 4

Lamb and noodle hotpot

2 garlic cloves, crushed
1 teaspoon Chinese five-spice
1 teaspoon sugar
3 cm (1¼ inch) piece fresh
   ginger, julienned
100 ml (3½ fl oz) Chinese rice
   wine
1 kg (2 lb 4 oz) boneless lamb
   shoulder, trimmed and cut
   into 3 cm (1¼ inch) pieces
30 g (1 oz) dried Chinese
   mushrooms
1 tablespoon oil
1 large onion, cut into wedges

2 teaspoons sichuan peppercorns,
   crushed or ground
2 tablespoons sweet bean paste
500 ml (17 fl oz/2 cups) chicken
   stock
3 tablespoons oyster sauce
2 star anise
80 g (2¾ oz) tin sliced bamboo
   shoots, drained
100 g (3½ oz) tin water
   chestnuts, drained and sliced
400 g (14 oz) wide rice noodles
1 spring onion (scallion), sliced

Put the garlic, five-spice, sugar, half the ginger, 2 tablespoons of the rice wine and 1 teaspoon salt in a large bowl. Marinate the lamb for 2 hours. Soak the mushrooms in boiling water for 20 minutes. Drain. Discard the stems and slice the caps.

Heat a wok over high heat, add the oil and swirl to coat. Stir-fry the onion, sichuan pepper and remaining ginger for 2 minutes. Cook the lamb in batches, stir-frying for 3 minutes each batch. Return to the wok, stir in the bean paste and cook for 3 minutes. Transfer to a 2 litre (70 fl oz/8 cup) flameproof hotpot or casserole dish.

Stir in the stock, oyster sauce, star anise and remaining rice wine and simmer, covered, over low heat for 1½ hours, or until the lamb is tender. Stir in the bamboo shoots and water chestnuts and cook for 20 minutes. Add the mushrooms and noodles, stirring until heated through. Sprinkle with the spring onion before serving.

SERVES 4

Lion's head meatballs

6 dried Chinese mushrooms
100 g (3½ oz) cellophane
noodles (mung bean
vermicelli)
600 g (1 lb 5 oz) minced
(ground) pork
1 egg white
4 garlic cloves, finely chopped
1 tablespoon finely grated fresh
ginger
1 tablespoon cornflour
(cornstarch)

1½ tablespoons Chinese rice
wine
6 spring onions (scallions),
thinly sliced
500 ml (17 fl oz/2 cups) chicken
stock
2 tablespoons oil
3 tablespoons light soy sauce
1 teaspoon sugar
400 g (14 oz) bok choy (pak
choy), halved lengthways
and leaves separated

Soak the mushrooms in boiling water for 20 minutes. Drain. Discard the stems and thinly slice the caps. Soak the noodles in boiling water for 3–4 minutes, or until soft. Drain, then rinse under cold water. Preheat the oven to 220°C (425°F/Gas 7).

Place the pork, egg white, garlic, ginger, cornflour, rice wine, two-thirds of the spring onion and a pinch of salt in a food processor. Using the pulse button, process until smooth and well combined. Divide into eight and shape into large balls.

Bring the stock to the boil, then remove from the heat and keep warm.

Heat the oil in a wok over high heat. Fry the meatballs in batches for 2 minutes each side, or until golden, but not cooked through. Drain on crumpled paper towels. Place the meatballs, mushrooms, soy sauce and sugar in a 2.5 litre (87 fl oz/ 10 cup) ovenproof hotpot or casserole dish and cover with the hot stock. Bake, covered, for 45 minutes. Add the bok choy and noodles and bake, covered, for 10 minutes. Sprinkle with the remaining spring onion and serve.

SERVES 4

Mongolian hotpot

250 g (9 oz) dried rice vermicelli
600 g (1 lb 5 oz) lamb backstrap
   or loin fillet, thinly sliced
   across the grain
4 spring onions (scallions), sliced
1.5 litres (52 fl oz/6 cups) light
   chicken stock
3 x 6 cm (1¼ x 2½ inch) piece
   fresh ginger, cut into 6 slices
2 tablespoons Chinese rice wine
300 g (10½ oz) silken firm tofu,
   cut into 1.5 cm (⅝ inch) cubes

300 g (10½ oz) Chinese broccoli
   (gai larn), cut into 4 cm
   (1½ inch) lengths
75 g (2½ oz/1⅔ cups) shredded
   Chinese cabbage (wong bok)

Sauce
4 tablespoons light soy sauce
2 tablespoons Chinese sesame
   paste
1 tablespoon Chinese rice wine
1 teaspoon chilli and garlic paste

Soak the vermicelli in boiling water for 5–7 minutes, or until soft. Drain well, then divide among six serving bowls. Top with the lamb slices and spring onion.

To make the sauce, combine the soy sauce, sesame paste, rice wine and the chilli and garlic paste in a bowl.

Put the stock, ginger and rice wine in a 2.5 litre (87 fl oz/10 cup) flameproof hotpot or casserole dish. Cover and bring to the boil over high heat. Add the tofu and vegetables and simmer, uncovered, for 1 minute, or until the broccoli has wilted. Divide the tofu, broccoli and cabbage among the serving bowls, then ladle in the hot stock. Drizzle a little of the sauce on top and serve the rest on the side.

SERVES 6

NOTES: Make sure the stock is hot enough to cook the thin slices of lamb.

Traditionally, this recipe would be cooked at the dinner table in a Chinese steamboat — an aluminium pot with a steam spout in the middle.

Miso soup with udon and tofu

1 teaspoon dashi granules
3 tablespoons red miso paste
2 tablespoons soy sauce
400 g (14 oz) fresh udon noodles, separated
400 g (14 oz) silken firm tofu, cubed
100 g (3½ oz) fresh shiitake mushrooms, sliced
500 g (1 lb 2 oz) baby bok choy (pak choy), leaves separated

Place the dashi, miso, soy sauce and 1.25 litres (44 fl oz/5 cups) water in a large saucepan and bring to the boil. Reduce the heat and simmer for 10 minutes.

Add the udon noodles and cook for 5 minutes, or until soft. Stir in the tofu, shiitake mushrooms and bok choy and cook for 3 minutes, or until the bok choy wilts.

SERVES 2–4

Vegetable ramen

375 g (13 oz) fresh ramen
noodles
1 tablespoon peanut oil
1 tablespoon finely chopped
fresh ginger
2 garlic cloves, crushed
150 g (5½ oz) oyster
mushrooms, halved
1 small zucchini (courgette),
sliced into thin rounds
1 leek, white and light green
part, halved lengthways and
thinly sliced
100 g (3½ oz) snow peas
(mangetout), halved on the
diagonal

100 g (3½ oz) fried tofu puffs,
cut into matchsticks
1.25 litres (44 fl oz/5 cups)
vegetable stock
1½ tablespoons white miso
paste
2 tablespoons light soy sauce
1 tablespoon mirin
90 g (3¼ oz/1 cup) bean sprouts
1 teaspoon sesame oil
4 spring onions (scallions),
thinly sliced
100 g (3½ oz) enoki mushrooms,
ends trimmed

Cook the noodles in a large saucepan of boiling water for 3 minutes, or until just tender. Drain, then rinse under cold water.

Heat the peanut oil in a large saucepan over medium heat, add the ginger, crushed garlic, oyster mushrooms, zucchini, leek, snow peas and tofu puffs, and stir-fry for 2 minutes. Add the stock and 300 ml (10½ fl oz) water and bring to the boil, then reduce the heat and simmer. Stir in the miso, soy sauce and mirin until heated through. Do not boil. Stir in the bean sprouts and sesame oil.

Place the noodles in the bottom of six serving bowls, then pour in the soup. Garnish with the spring onion and enoki mushrooms.

SERVES 6

Long and short noodle soup

300 g (10½ oz) minced (ground) pork
3 garlic cloves, roughly chopped
2 teaspoons grated fresh ginger
2 teaspoons cornflour (cornstarch)
6 spring onions (scallions), sliced
125 ml (4 fl oz/½ cup) light soy sauce
3 tablespoons Chinese rice wine
30 won ton wrappers
3 litres (105 fl oz/12 cups) ready-made Chinese chicken broth or chicken stock
200 g (7 oz) dried flat egg noodles
1 teaspoon sesame oil

Put the pork, garlic, ginger, cornflour, most of the spring onion, 1½ tablespoons of the soy sauce and 1 tablespoon of the rice wine in a food processor and process until well combined. Place 2 teaspoons of the mixture in the centre of a won ton wrapper and lightly brush the edges with water. Lift the sides up tightly and pinch around the filling to form a pouch. Repeat this process to make 30 won tons.

Place the chicken broth in a large saucepan and bring to a simmer over medium–high heat. Stir in the remaining soy sauce and rice wine.

Meanwhile, bring a large saucepan of water to the boil. Reduce the heat, add the won tons and simmer for 1 minute, or until they float to the surface and are cooked through, then remove with a slotted spoon. Return to the boil, add the noodles and cook for 3 minutes, or until tender. Drain and add to the broth along with the cooked won tons. Simmer for 2 minutes, or until heated through.

Divide the broth, noodles and won tons among six large serving bowls, sprinkle with the remaining spring onion and drizzle each with a little sesame oil.

SERVES 6

Pork and cellophane noodle soup

150 g (5½ oz) cellophane noodles (mung bean vermicelli)
2 teaspoons oil
2 teaspoons grated fresh ginger
1.25 litres (44 fl oz/5 cups) chicken stock
4 tablespoons Chinese rice wine
1 tablespoon hoisin sauce
1 tablespoon soy sauce
4 spring onions (scallions), thinly sliced on the diagonal,
    plus extra, to garnish
300 g (10½ oz) Chinese barbecued pork (char siu), sliced

Soak the noodles in boiling water for 3–4 minutes, or until soft. Drain, then rinse under cold water.

Heat the oil in a large saucepan. Add the ginger and stir-fry for 1 minute. Add the stock, Chinese rice wine, hoisin and soy sauce and simmer for 10 minutes. Add the spring onion and pork, then cook for a further 5 minutes.

Divide the noodles among four large bowls, ladle in the soup and arrange the pork on top. Garnish with extra spring onion.

SERVES 4

Japanese beef, tofu and noodle soup

10 g (¼ oz) dried sliced shiitake
    mushrooms
100 g (3½ oz) dried rice
    vermicelli
2 teaspoons oil
1 leek, halved and sliced
1 litre (35 fl oz/4 cups) chicken
    stock
1 teaspoon dashi granules
    dissolved in 500 ml (17 fl oz/
    2 cups) boiling water

125 ml (4 fl oz/½ cup) soy sauce
2 tablespoons mirin
1½ tablespoons sugar
90 g (3¼ oz/2 cups) shredded
    Chinese cabbage (wong bok)
300 g (10½ oz) silken firm tofu,
    cut into 2 cm (¾ inch) cubes
600 g (1 lb 5 oz) rump steak,
    thinly sliced
4 spring onions (scallions), sliced
    on the diagonal

Soak the shiitake mushrooms in 125 ml (4 fl oz/½ cup) boiling water for 10 minutes. Soak the vermicelli in boiling water for 5–7 minutes, or until soft. Drain the noodles.

Heat the oil in a large saucepan, add the leek and cook over medium heat for 3 minutes, or until softened. Add the chicken stock, dashi broth, soy sauce, mirin, sugar and mushrooms and their soaking liquid. Bring to the boil, then reduce the heat and simmer for 5 minutes.

Add the cabbage and simmer for a further 5 minutes. Next, add the tofu and beef and simmer for 5 minutes, or until the beef is cooked but still tender. Divide the noodles among the serving bowls and ladle in the soup. Serve garnished with the spring onion slices.

SERVES 4–6

Tofu puffs with mushrooms and round rice noodles

8 dried shiitake mushrooms
500 g (1 lb 2 oz) fresh round
  rice noodles
3 litres (105 fl oz/12 cups)
  chicken stock
1 carrot, thinly sliced on the
  diagonal
100 g (3½ oz) fried tofu puffs,
  halved

800 g (1 lb 12 oz) bok choy (pak
  choy), trimmed and quartered
1–1½ tablespoons mushroom
  soy sauce
6 drops sesame oil
ground white pepper, to season
100 g (3½ oz) enoki mushrooms,
  ends trimmed

Soak the shiitake mushrooms in boiling water for 20 minutes. Drain, then discard the stems. Meanwhile, briefly soak the noodles in boiling water. Gently separate the noodles, then drain well.

Place the chicken stock in a large saucepan, cover and slowly heat over low heat.

Add the noodles to the simmering stock along with the carrot, tofu puffs, shiitake mushrooms and bok choy. Cook for 1–2 minutes, or until the carrot and noodles are tender and the bok choy has wilted slightly. Stir in the soy sauce and sesame oil and season to taste with white pepper.

Divide the noodles, vegetables, tofu puffs and enoki mushrooms among four serving bowls, ladle the broth on top and serve immediately.

SERVES 4

Ramen noodle soup with pork and greens

15 g (½ oz) dried shiitake mushrooms
350 g (12 oz) Chinese broccoli (gai larn),
    trimmed and cut into 4 cm (1½ inch) lengths
375 g (13 oz) fresh ramen noodles
1.5 litres (52 fl oz/6 cups) chicken stock
3 tablespoons soy sauce
1 teaspoon sugar
350 g (12 oz) Chinese barbecued pork (char siu),
    thinly sliced
1 small red chilli, seeded and thinly sliced

Soak the mushrooms in 125 ml (4 fl oz/½ cup) boiling water for 20 minutes. Drain, reserving the liquid. Discard the stems and thinly slice the caps.

Blanch the broccoli in a large saucepan of boiling salted water for 3 minutes, or until tender but firm to the bite. Drain, then refresh in cold water.

Cook the noodles in a large saucepan of boiling water for 3 minutes, or until just tender. Drain, then rinse under cold water. Set aside.

Place the stock in a large saucepan and bring to the boil. Add the sliced mushrooms and reserved mushroom liquid, soy sauce and sugar. Simmer for 2 minutes, then add the broccoli.

Divide the noodles among four large bowls. Ladle on the hot stock and vegetables. Top with the pork and sliced chilli. Serve hot.

SERVES 4

Crab and corn eggflower noodle broth

75 g (2½ oz) dried thin egg
 noodles
1 tablespoon oil
1 teaspoon finely chopped fresh
 ginger
3 spring onions (scallions),
 thinly sliced, white and
 green parts separated
1.25 litres (44 fl oz/5 cups)
 chicken stock
250 g (9 oz) baby corn, sliced
 on the diagonal into 1 cm
 (½ inch) thick slices

4 tablespoons mirin
175 g (6 oz) fresh cooked
 crabmeat
1 tablespoon cornflour
 (cornstarch) mixed with
 1 tablespoon water
2 eggs, lightly beaten
2 teaspoons lime juice
1 tablespoon soy sauce
3 tablespoons torn coriander
 (cilantro) leaves

Cook the noodles in a large saucepan of boiling water for 3 minutes, or until tender. Drain, then rinse under cold water.

Heat the oil in a large heavy-based saucepan. Add the ginger and the spring onion (white part) and cook over medium heat for 1–2 minutes. Add the stock, corn and mirin and bring to the boil. Simmer for about 5 minutes. Stir in the noodles, crabmeat and cornflour mixture. Return to a simmer, stirring constantly until it thickens. Reduce the heat and pour in the egg in a thin stream, stirring constantly — do not boil. Gently stir in the lime juice, soy sauce and half the coriander.

Divide the noodles among four bowls and ladle the soup on top. Garnish with the spring onion (green part) and remaining coriander leaves.

SERVES 4

Green tea noodle soup

200 g (7 oz) dried green tea noodles
2 teaspoons dashi granules
1 tablespoon mirin
1 tablespoon Japanese soy sauce
200 g (7 oz) firm tofu, drained and cut
    into 1.5 cm (⅝ inch) cubes
1 nori sheet, shredded
3 teaspoons sesame seeds, toasted

Cook the noodles in a large saucepan of boiling salted water for 5 minutes, or until tender. Drain, then rinse under cold water.

Combine the dashi granules with 1.5 litres (52 fl oz/6 cups) water in a large saucepan. Stir over medium–high heat until the granules have dissolved. Increase the heat to high and bring to the boil. Stir in the mirin and soy sauce.

Divide the noodles and tofu cubes among four serving bowls and ladle the hot stock on top. Garnish with the nori and sesame seeds. Serve immediately.

SERVES 4

Shabu shabu

300 g (10½ oz) beef fillet,
trimmed
1.5 litres (52 fl oz/6 cups)
chicken stock
2 x 6 cm (¾ x 2½ inch) piece
fresh ginger, thinly sliced
4 tablespoons light soy sauce
2 tablespoons mirin
1 teaspoon sesame oil
200 g (7 oz) fresh udon noodles
150 g (5½ oz) English spinach
leaves, thinly sliced

400 g (14 oz) Chinese cabbage
(wong bok) leaves, finely
shredded
100 g (3½ oz) fresh shiitake
mushrooms, stems removed
and caps thinly sliced
200 g (7 oz) firm tofu, cut into
2 cm (¾ inch) cubes
4 tablespoons ponzu sauce (see
Note page 17)

Wrap the beef fillet in plastic wrap and freeze for 40 minutes, or until it begins to harden. Remove and slice as thinly as possible across the grain.

Place the stock, ginger, soy sauce, mirin and sesame oil in a 2.5 litre (87 fl oz/10 cup) flameproof casserole dish or hotpot over medium heat and simmer for 3 minutes. Add the noodles, gently stir with chopsticks to separate them, and cook for 1–2 minutes. Add the spinach, cabbage, mushrooms and tofu and simmer for 1 minute, or until the leaves have wilted.

Divide the noodles among four bowls using tongs, and top with the beef, vegetables and tofu. Ladle the hot stock on top and serve the ponzu sauce on the side.

SERVES 4

NOTE: Traditionally, raw beef slices are arranged on a plate with the mushrooms, vegetables, tofu and noodles. The stock and seasoning are heated on a portable gas flame at the table. Guests cook the meat and vegetables in the stock and dip them into the sauce. The noodles are added at the end and served with the broth.

Fish hotpot with ginger and tomatoes

1 tablespoon oil
1 onion, cut into thin wedges
1 small red chilli, sliced
3 garlic cloves, finely chopped
2 x 2 cm (¾ x ¾ inch) piece fresh ginger, julienned
½ teaspoon ground turmeric
400 g (14 oz) tin chopped tomatoes
1 litre (35 fl oz/4 cups) chicken stock
1 tablespoon tamarind purée
85 g (3 oz) dried flat rice noodle sticks
600 g (1 lb 5 oz) snapper fillets, skin removed,
    cut into 3 cm (1¼ inch) cubes
coriander (cilantro) leaves, to garnish

Preheat the oven to 220°C (425°F/Gas 7). Heat the oil in a frying pan over medium–high heat and cook the onion for 1–2 minutes, or until soft. Add the chilli, garlic and ginger and cook for a further 30 seconds. Add the turmeric, tomatoes, chicken stock and tamarind purée and bring to the boil over high heat. Transfer to a 2.5 litre (87 fl oz/10 cup) ovenproof hotpot or casserole dish and cook, covered, in the oven for 40 minutes.

Soak the noodles in warm water for 15–20 minutes, or until tender. Drain and rinse.

Remove the hotpot from the oven and stir in the noodles. Add the fish cubes, then cover and return to the oven for a further 10 minutes, or until the fish is cooked through. Serve sprinkled with some coriander leaves.

SERVES 4

Asian vegetarian noodle soup

8 dried Chinese mushrooms
100 g (3½ oz) dried rice vermicelli
800 g (1 lb 12 oz) Chinese broccoli (gai larn),
    cut into 5 cm (2 inch) lengths
8 fried tofu puffs, cut into strips
125 g (4½ oz) bean sprouts
1 litre (35 fl oz/4 cups) vegetable stock
2 tablespoons light soy sauce
1½ tablespoons Chinese rice wine
3 spring onions (scallions), finely chopped
coriander (cilantro) leaves, to serve

Soak the mushrooms in 125 ml (4 fl oz/½ cup) boiling water for 20 minutes. Drain, reserving the liquid. Discard the stems and thinly slice the caps.

Soak the vermicelli in boiling water for 5–7 minutes, or until soft. Drain. Divide the vermicelli, broccoli, tofu puffs and bean sprouts among the four serving bowls.

Place the reserved mushroom liquid, stock, soy sauce, rice wine, spring onion and mushrooms in a saucepan and bring to the boil. Cook, covered, for 10 minutes.

Ladle the soup into the serving bowls and garnish with the coriander leaves.

SERVES 4

Eight treasure noodle soup

10 g (¼ oz) dried shiitake
    mushrooms
375 g (13 oz) fresh thick egg
    noodles
1.25 litres (44 fl oz/5 cups)
    chicken stock
3 tablespoons light soy sauce
2 teaspoons Chinese rice wine
200 g (7 oz) boneless, skinless
    chicken breast, cut into 1 cm
    (½ inch) thick strips

200 g (7 oz) Chinese barbecued
    pork (char siu), cut into
    5 mm (¼ inch) thick slices
¼ onion, finely chopped
1 carrot, cut into 1 cm (½ inch)
    thick slices on the diagonal
125 g (4½ oz) snow peas
    (mangetout), halved on the
    diagonal
4 spring onions (scallions),
    thinly sliced

Soak the mushrooms in boiling water for 20 minutes. Drain. Discard the stems and thinly slice the caps.

Cook the noodles in a large saucepan of boiling water for 1 minute. Drain, then rinse under cold water. Divide among four warmed serving bowls.

Meanwhile, bring the chicken stock to the boil in a large saucepan over high heat. Reduce the heat to medium and add the soy sauce and rice wine, stirring to combine. Simmer for 2 minutes. Add the chicken and pork and cook for another 2 minutes, or until the chicken is cooked through and the pork is heated. Add the onion, carrot, snow peas, shiitake mushrooms and half the spring onion and cook for a further 1 minute, or until the carrot is tender.

Divide the vegetables and meat among the serving bowls and ladle on the hot broth. Garnish each bowl with the remaining spring onion.

SERVES 4

Pork and buttered corn ramen soup

200 g (7 oz) Chinese barbecued
    pork (char siu) fillet in one
    piece
2 small fresh corn cobs (550 g/
    1 lb 4 oz)
200 g (7 oz) dried ramen noodles
2 teaspoons oil
1 teaspoon grated fresh ginger

1.5 litres (52 fl oz/6 cups)
    chicken stock
2 tablespoons mirin
2 spring onions (scallions),
    sliced on the diagonal
20 g (¾ oz) unsalted butter
1 spring onion (scallion), extra,
    sliced on the diagonal

Cut the pork into thin slices and remove the corn kernels from the cob using a sharp knife.

Cook the noodles in a large saucepan of boiling water for 5 minutes, or until tender. Drain, then rinse under cold water.

Heat the oil in a large saucepan over high heat. Stir-fry the grated ginger for 1 minute. Add the chicken stock and mirin and bring to the boil. Reduce the heat and simmer for 8 minutes.

Add the pork slices to the liquid and cook for 5 minutes, then add the corn kernels and spring onion and cook for a further 4–5 minutes, or until the kernels are tender.

Separate the noodles by running them under hot water, then divide among four deep bowls. Ladle on the soup, then place 1 teaspoon butter on each serving. Garnish with the extra spring onion and serve at once.

SERVES 4

NOTE: This soup is traditionally served with the butter on top. However, for a healthier option, it can be eaten without the butter.

Vegetarian laksa

200 g (7 oz) dried rice vermicelli
2 tablespoons oil
2–3 tablespoons laksa paste
1 litre (35 fl oz/4 cups) vegetable stock
750 ml (26 fl oz/3 cups) coconut milk
250 g (9 oz) snowpeas (mangetout), halved on the diagonal
5 spring onions (scallions), cut into 3 cm (1¼ inch) lengths
2 tablespoons lime juice
125 g (4½ oz) bean sprouts
200 g (7 oz) fried tofu puffs, halved
3 tablespoons roughly chopped Vietnamese mint
1 large handful coriander (cilantro) leaves

Soak the vermicelli in boiling water for 5–7 minutes, or until soft.

Meanwhile, heat the oil in a large saucepan, add the laksa paste and cook, stirring, over medium heat for 1 minute, or until fragrant. Add the stock, coconut milk, snowpeas and spring onion and simmer for 5 minutes. Pour in the lime juice and season to taste with salt and freshly ground black pepper.

Drain the vermicelli and divide among four bowls. Top with the bean sprouts and fried tofu puffs. Ladle the hot soup into the bowls and sprinkle with the fresh mint and coriander. Serve immediately.

SERVES 4

Thai mussels with noodles

2 kg (4 lb 8 oz) mussels
235 g (8½ oz) cellophane noodles (mung bean vermicelli)
2 garlic cloves, crushed
2 spring onions (scallions), finely chopped
2 tablespoons red curry paste
160 ml (5¼ fl oz) coconut cream
juice of 2 limes
2 tablespoons fish sauce
1 handful coriander (cilantro) leaves

Rinse the mussels in cold water and pull off any beards. Now look at each one individually and, if it isn't tightly closed, tap it on the work surface to see if it will close. Throw away any mussels that won't close.

Soak the noodles in boiling water for 3–4 minutes, or until soft. Drain, then rinse under cold water. Cut them into short lengths with scissors.

Put the mussels in a deep frying pan or wok with the garlic and spring onion and 125 ml (4 fl oz/½ cup) water. Bring to the boil, then cover and cook the mussels for 2–3 minutes, shaking occasionally, or until they are all open. Throw away any that don't open. Tip the whole lot, including any liquid, into a sieve lined with a piece of muslin (cheesecloth), reserving the liquid.

Pour the cooking liquid back into the pan, add the curry paste and coconut cream and stir together. Bring the mixture to the boil, then add the lime juice and fish sauce. Put the mussels back in the pan. Cook for a minute, then stir in the coriander leaves.

Put some noodles in each bowl and ladle the mussels on top.

SERVES 4

Chiang mai noodles

250 g (9 oz) fresh thin egg
noodles
2 tablespoons oil
6 red Asian shallots, finely
chopped
3 garlic cloves, crushed
1–2 small red chillies, seeded
and finely chopped
2–3 tablespoons red curry paste
375 g (13 oz) boneless, skinless
chicken breast, thinly sliced
2 tablespoons fish sauce
1 tablespoon grated palm sugar
(jaggery) or soft brown sugar

750 ml (26 fl oz/3 cups) coconut
milk
1 tablespoon lime juice
250 ml (9 fl oz/1 cup) chicken
stock
4 spring onions (scallions),
sliced, to garnish
4 tablespoons coriander
(cilantro) leaves, to garnish
fried red Asian shallot flakes,
to garnish
purchased fried noodles,
to garnish
finely diced red chilli, to garnish

Cook the noodles in a large saucepan of boiling water for 1 minute, or until tender.
Drain, then set aside.

Heat a large wok over high heat, add the oil and swirl to coat. Add the shallots, garlic
and chilli, and stir-fry for 3 minutes. Stir in the curry paste and stir-fry for 2 minutes.
Add the chicken and stir-fry for 3 minutes, or until it changes colour.

Stir in the fish sauce, palm sugar, coconut milk, lime juice and stock. Reduce the
heat and simmer over low heat for 5 minutes — do not boil.

To serve, divide the noodles among four deep serving bowls and spoon in the
chicken mixture. Garnish with the spring onion, coriander, shallot flakes, noodles
and diced chilli.

SERVES 4

crunch

Prawn and rice noodle salad

250 g (9 oz) rice stick noodles
700 g (1 lb 9 oz) medium cooked
    prawns (shrimp), peeled and
    deveined, tails intact
1 carrot, coarsely grated
1 small Lebanese (short)
    cucumber, thinly sliced
3 handfuls coriander (cilantro)
    leaves
80 g (2¾ oz/½ cup) chopped
    roasted unsalted peanuts
50 g (1¾ oz) crisp fried shallots

Dressing
125 ml (4 fl oz/½ cup) rice
    vinegar
1 tablespoon grated palm sugar
    (jaggery) or soft brown sugar
1 garlic clove, finely chopped
2 red chillies, finely chopped
3 tablespoons fish sauce
3 tablespoons lime juice
2 tablespoons oil

Soak the noodles in boiling water for 10 minutes. Drain, then rinse under cold water. Place in a large serving bowl.

Add the prawns, carrot, cucumber and coriander to the bowl and toss.

To make the dressing, combine the vinegar, sugar and garlic in a small saucepan and bring to the boil, then reduce the heat and simmer for 3 minutes to slightly reduce the liquid. Transfer to a bowl and add the chilli, fish sauce and lime juice. Slowly whisk in the oil, and season to taste.

Toss the dressing through the salad, then scatter with the peanuts and crisp fried shallots and serve.

SERVES 4

Thai chicken with cellophane noodles

4 tablespoons coconut cream
1 tablespoon fish sauce
1 tablespoon grated palm sugar
(jaggery) or soft brown sugar
2 boneless, skinless chicken
breasts, thinly sliced
120 g (4¼ oz) cellophane
noodles (mung bean
vermicelli)
2 lemongrass stems
4 makrut (kaffir lime) leaves

1 red onion, finely chopped
1 large handful coriander
(cilantro) leaves, chopped
1 large handful mint, chopped
1–2 red chillies, sliced
3 green bird's eye chillies, thinly
sliced
2 tablespoons roasted peanuts,
chopped
1–2 limes, halved or quartered

Put the coconut cream, fish sauce and palm sugar in a small saucepan and bring to the boil, then add the chicken and simmer for about 1 minute, or until the chicken is cooked through, stirring occasionally. Leave the chicken to cool in the sauce. Soak the noodles in boiling water for 3–4 minutes, or until soft. Drain, then rinse under cold water. Cut them into short lengths with scissors.

Peel the lemongrass until you reach the first purplish ring, then trim off the root. Make two or three cuts down through the bulb-like root, thinly slice across it until it starts to get harder, then throw the hard top piece away. Pull the stems out of the lime leaves by folding the leaves in half, with the shiny side inwards, and pulling down on the stalk. Roll up the leaves tightly, then slice them very finely across.

Put all the ingredients in a bowl with the noodles and chicken, with its sauce, and toss everything together.

SERVES 4

Lamb and rice noodle salad with peanut dressing

500 g (1 lb 2 oz) lamb fillet,
thinly sliced lengthways
2 tablespoons light soy sauce
1 tablespoon Chinese rice wine
125 g (4½ oz) dried rice noodle
sticks
1 telegraph (long) cucumber,
unpeeled, cut into long thin
strips with a vegetable peeler
100 g (3½ oz) chopped
unsalted toasted peanuts
coriander (cilantro) sprigs, to
garnish

Spicy peanut dressing
3 garlic cloves
175 g (6 oz) smooth peanut
butter
4 tablespoons soy sauce
3 handfuls coriander (cilantro)
leaves
1 tablespoon rice vinegar
1 tablespoon Chinese rice wine
2 tablespoons grated palm sugar
(jaggery) or soft brown sugar
1 small red chilli, roughly
chopped

Combine the lamb, soy sauce and rice wine in a bowl. Cover and marinate for 1 hour.

To make the peanut dressing, purée all the ingredients with 2 tablespoons water in a blender until smooth.

Soak the noodles in a bowl of boiling water for 15 minutes. Drain, then rinse under cold water.

Heat a chargrill pan or grill (broiler) to very hot and sear the lamb slices in batches for 30 seconds on each side, or until cooked to your liking, then transfer to a large bowl. Add the noodles, cucumber and three-quarters of the dressing and toss to combine. Drizzle with the remaining dressing, scatter with the peanuts, garnish with the coriander sprigs and serve.

SERVES 4

Tuna and coriander noodle salad

Dressing
3 tablespoons lime juice
2 tablespoons fish sauce
2 tablespoons sweet chilli sauce
2 teaspoons grated palm sugar
    (jaggery) or soft brown sugar
1 teaspoon sesame oil
1 garlic clove, finely chopped

1 tablespoon virgin olive oil
4 tuna steaks, at room
    temperature
200 g (7 oz) dried thin wheat
    noodles
6 spring onions (scallions),
    thinly sliced
3 handfuls coriander (cilantro)
    leaves, chopped
lime wedges, to garnish

To make the dressing, place the lime juice, fish sauce, chilli sauce, sugar, sesame oil and garlic in a small bowl and mix together.

Heat the olive oil in a chargrill pan. Add the tuna steaks and cook over high heat for 2 minutes each side, or until cooked to your liking. Transfer the steaks to a warm plate, cover and keep warm.

Place the noodles in a large saucepan of rapidly boiling lightly salted water and return to the boil. Cook for 4 minutes, or until the noodles are tender. Drain well. Add half the dressing and half the spring onion and coriander to the noodles and gently toss together.

Either cut the tuna into even cubes or slice it. Place the noodles on serving plates and top with the tuna. Mix the remaining dressing with the spring onion and coriander and drizzle over the tuna. Garnish with lime wedges.

SERVES 4

Roast duck and noodle salad

400 g (14 oz) fresh flat egg
    noodles
1 teaspoon sesame oil, plus
    1 tablespoon extra
1 tablespoon grated fresh ginger
½–1 teaspoon sambal oelek,
    or to taste
2 tablespoons fish sauce
2 tablespoons rice vinegar
1 tablespoon lime juice
¼ teaspoon Chinese five-spice
1 tablespoon soft brown sugar

2 tablespoons peanut oil
50 g (1¾ oz/1 cup) roughly
    chopped coriander (cilantro),
    plus extra leaves, to garnish
1 Chinese roast duck, meat
    removed from bones and
    sliced into bite-sized pieces
180 g (6 oz/2 cups) bean sprouts
3 spring onions (scallions),
    thinly sliced
80 g (2¾ oz/½ cup) chopped
    roasted peanuts

Cook the noodles in a large saucepan of boiling water for 3–4 minutes, or until just tender. Drain, then rinse under cold water. Toss with 1 teaspoon sesame oil.

Place the ginger, sambal oelek, fish sauce, vinegar, lime juice, five-spice and sugar in a small bowl and stir to dissolve the sugar. Whisk in the extra sesame oil and the peanut oil, then stir in the coriander. Season to taste with salt.

Place the noodles, duck, bean sprouts and spring onion in a large bowl. Pour on the dressing and toss to coat. Season to taste. Garnish with the chopped peanuts and extra coriander leaves.

SERVES 4

Buckwheat noodle and sweet and sour capsicum salad

3 capsicums (peppers), preferably
   red, green and yellow
2 tablespoons peanut oil
5 teaspoons sesame oil
2 star anise
3 tablespoons red wine vinegar
1 tablespoon fish sauce
125 g (4½ oz) sugar

300 g (10½ oz) dried soba
   (buckwheat) noodles
½ tablespoon balsamic vinegar
½ teaspoon sugar, extra
2 spring onions (scallions),
   thinly sliced
2 tablespoons sesame seeds,
   lightly toasted

Thinly slice the capsicums. Heat the peanut oil and 1 teaspoon of the sesame oil in a saucepan over medium heat. Cook the star anise for 1 minute, or until the oil begins to smoke. Add the capsicum and stir for 2 minutes. Reduce the heat to low and cook, covered, for 5 minutes, stirring occasionally. Increase to medium heat and add the vinegar, fish sauce and sugar, stirring until dissolved. Boil for 2 minutes, then remove from the heat and cool. Remove the star anise. Drain and place the capsicum in a bowl.

Cook the noodles in a large saucepan of boiling water for 5 minutes, or until tender. Drain, then rinse under cold water.

Combine the balsamic vinegar, remaining sesame oil, extra sugar and ½ teaspoon salt, stirring until the sugar dissolves. Add the noodles and toss to coat, then combine with the capsicum and spring onion. Sprinkle with the sesame seeds and serve.

SERVES 4

Pork and udon noodle salad with lime dressing

Dressing
4 tablespoons lime juice
1 tablespoon sesame oil
2 tablespoons ponzu
3 tablespoons honey

400 g (14 oz) fresh udon noodles
500 g (1 lb 2 oz) pork fillet
1 tablespoon sesame oil
200 g (7 oz) roasted unsalted peanuts

2 large red chillies, seeded and finely diced
2 teaspoons finely chopped fresh ginger
1 telegraph (long) cucumber, peeled, halved, seeds removed and julienned
200 g (7 oz) bean sprouts
1 large handful coriander (cilantro) leaves, chopped

Preheat the oven to 200°C (400°F/Gas 6). To make the dressing, place the lime juice, sesame oil, ponzu and honey in a screwtop jar and shake.

Cook the noodles in a saucepan of boiling water for 1–2 minutes, or until tender. Drain, rinse under cold water and set aside.

Trim any fat and sinew off the pork and brush with the sesame oil. Season. Heat a non-stick frying pan until very hot and cook the pork for 5–6 minutes, or until browned on all sides and cooked to your liking. Remove from the pan and rest for 5 minutes.

Combine the noodles, peanuts, chilli, ginger, cucumber, bean sprouts and coriander and toss well. Cut the pork into thin slices, add to the salad with the dressing and toss before serving.

SERVES 4

Spice-crusted salmon and noodle salad

Dressing
½ teaspoon wasabi paste
4 tablespoons Japanese soy sauce
5 tablespoons mirin
1 teaspoon sugar

250 g (9 oz) dried somen noodles
1 teaspoon sesame oil
1 teaspoon sansho powder (see Note)

1 tablespoon peanut oil
3 salmon fillets (about 200 g/ 7 oz each), skin removed
4 spring onions (scallions), thinly sliced on the diagonal
2 handfuls coriander (cilantro) leaves
1 Lebanese (short) cucumber, halved lengthways, thinly sliced

To make the dressing, combine the wasabi with a little of the soy sauce to form a smooth paste. Stir in the mirin, sugar and remaining soy sauce.

Cook the noodles in a large saucepan of boiling water for 2 minutes, or until tender. Drain, then rinse under cold water. Transfer to a large bowl and toss with the sesame oil.

Combine the sansho powder, peanut oil and ¼ teaspoon salt and brush over both sides of the salmon. Heat a large frying pan over medium heat. Add the salmon and cook each side for 2–3 minutes, or until cooked to your liking. Remove from the pan and flake into large pieces with a fork. Add the salmon, spring onion, coriander, cucumber and half the dressing to the noodles, then toss together. Transfer to a serving dish and drizzle with the remaining dressing.

SERVES 4

NOTE: Sansho powder is available from Japanese food stores.

Pork, prawn and vermicelli salad in lettuce cups

oil, for deep-frying
100 g (3½ oz) dried rice
   vermicelli
3 tablespoons peanut oil
1 garlic clove, crushed
1 tablespoon finely chopped
   fresh ginger
3 spring onions (scallions),
   thinly sliced and green ends
   reserved for garnish
150 g (5½ oz) minced (ground)
   pork

500 g (1 lb 2 oz) raw prawns
   (shrimp), peeled, deveined
   and roughly chopped
2 tablespoons Chinese rice wine
2 tablespoons soy sauce
2 tablespoons hoisin sauce
1 tablespoon brown bean sauce
½ teaspoon sugar
3 tablespoons chicken stock
12 iceberg lettuce leaves,
   trimmed into cups

Fill a wok or deep heavy-based saucepan one-third full of oil and heat to 170°C (325°F), or until a cube of bread browns in 20 seconds. Add the vermicelli in batches and deep-fry until puffed up but not browned — this will only take a few seconds. Remove with a slotted spoon and drain on crumpled paper towels.

Heat the peanut oil in a wok over high heat and swirl to coat the side. Add the garlic, ginger and spring onion, and stir-fry for 1 minute. Add the pork, breaking up the lumps, and cook for 4 minutes. Add the prawns and stir-fry for 2 minutes.

Add the rice wine, soy, hoisin and brown bean sauces, sugar, stock and ½ teaspoon salt and stir until combined. Cook over high heat for 2 minutes, or until the mixture thickens slightly. Divide the noodles among the lettuce cups, top with the pork and prawn mixture and garnish with the reserved spring onion. Serve immediately.

SERVES 6

Asian salmon and noodle salad

125 ml (4 fl oz/½ cup) lime juice
2 tablespoons grated fresh
    ginger
500 g (1 lb 2 oz) fresh salmon
    fillet, skinned, bones
    removed, thinly sliced
600 g (1 lb 5 oz) fresh egg
    noodles
2 tablespoons mirin
2 tablespoons fish sauce
2 teaspoons grated palm sugar
    (jaggery) or soft brown sugar

3 tablespoons peanut oil
2 teaspoons sesame oil
1 small red chilli, chopped
8 spring onions (scallions), sliced
2 tablespoons coriander
    (cilantro) leaves
1 tablespoon Vietnamese mint,
    finely chopped
2 tablespoons chopped Chinese
    garlic chives
coriander (cilantro) leaves,
    to garnish

Combine the lime juice and ginger in a bowl, add the salmon and toss to coat. Refrigerate for up to 2 hours.

Cook the noodles in a large saucepan of boiling water for 2–3 minutes. Drain, then rinse under cold water.

Remove the fish from the marinade. Add the mirin, fish sauce, palm sugar, peanut and sesame oils, and chilli to the marinade. Mix well. Place the noodles, fish, spring onion and fresh herbs in a large bowl, add the dressing and toss to coat. Garnish with the coriander leaves.

SERVES 4

Idiyappam

225 g (8 oz) dried rice noodle
sticks or dried rice vermicelli
4 tablespoons oil
4 tablespoons cashew nuts
½ onion, chopped
3 eggs
155 g (5½ oz/1 cup) fresh or
frozen peas

10 curry leaves
2 carrots, grated
2 leeks, finely shredded
1 red capsicum (pepper), diced
2 tablespoons tomato sauce
(ketchup)
1 tablespoon soy sauce
1 teaspoon salt

Soak the rice noodle sticks in cold water for 30 minutes, then drain and put them in a saucepan of boiling water. Remove from the heat and leave in the pan for 3 minutes. Drain and refresh under cold water.

Heat 1 tablespoon of the oil in a frying pan and fry the cashews until golden. Remove, add the onion to the pan, fry until dark golden, then drain on paper towels. Cook the eggs in boiling water for 10 minutes until hard-boiled, then cool immediately in cold water. When cold, peel them and cut into wedges. Cook the peas in boiling water until tender.

Heat the remaining oil in a frying pan and briefly fry the curry leaves. Add the carrot, leek and capsicum and stir for 1 minute. Add the tomato sauce, soy sauce, salt and noodle sticks and mix, stirring constantly to prevent the noodle sticks from sticking to the pan. Serve on a platter and garnish with the peas, cashews, fried onion and egg wedges.

SERVES 4

Vietnamese salad with lemongrass dressing

200 g (7 oz) dried rice vermicelli
1 large handful Vietnamese
  mint, torn
1 large handful coriander
  (cilantro) leaves
½ red onion, cut into thin
  wedges
1 green mango, cut into
  julienne strips
1 Lebanese (short) cucumber,
  halved lengthways and
  thinly sliced on the diagonal
140 g (5 oz/1 cup) crushed
  peanuts

Lemongrass dressing
125 ml (4 fl oz/½ cup) lime juice
1 tablespoon grated palm sugar
  (jaggery) or soft brown sugar
3 tablespoons seasoned rice
  vinegar
2 lemongrass stems, white part
  only, finely chopped
2 red chillies, seeded and finely
  chopped
3 makrut (kaffir) lime leaves,
  shredded

Soak the vermicelli in boiling water for 5–7 minutes, or until soft. Drain, rinse under cold water and cut into short lengths with scissors.

Place the vermicelli, mint, coriander, onion, mango, cucumber and three-quarters of the nuts in a large bowl and toss together.

To make the dressing, place all the ingredients in a jar with a lid and shake together.

Toss the dressing through the salad and refrigerate for 30 minutes. Sprinkle with the remaining nuts just before serving.

SERVES 4–6

Rare beef fillet with cellophane noodles and ginger dressing

400 g (14 oz) top-grade beef
   fillet, trimmed
2 tablespoons peanut oil
250 g (9 oz) cellophane noodles
   (mung bean vermicelli)
½ teaspoon sesame oil
2 spring onions (scallions),
   thinly sliced on the diagonal

Ginger dressing
1½ tablespoons finely chopped
   fresh ginger
3 tablespoons light soy sauce
3 tablespoons mirin
1 teaspoon sugar
2 teaspoons rice vinegar

Season the beef with black pepper. Heat the peanut oil in a large frying pan. When very hot, sear the meat in batches on all sides for 3 minutes, or until brown but pink on the inside. Cool slightly, then cover and refrigerate until cold.

Soak the noodles in boiling water for 3–4 minutes, or until soft. Drain, then rinse under cold water. Return to the bowl, add the sesame oil and toss well together.

To make the ginger dressing, combine the chopped ginger in a small bowl with the other ingredients, stirring until the sugar has completely dissolved.

Add half the spring onion to the bowl of noodles, toss well, then place on a platter. Cut the beef into thin slices, then arrange on top of the noodles.

Warm the dressing slightly over low heat, then pour over the beef and noodles. Scatter with the remaining spring onion and serve immediately.

SERVES 4

Crab and spinach soba noodle salad

3 tablespoons Japanese rice vinegar
125 ml (4 fl oz/½ cup) mirin
2 tablespoons soy sauce
1 teaspoon finely chopped fresh ginger
400 g (14 oz) English spinach leaves
250 g (9 oz) fresh cooked crabmeat
250 g (9 oz) dried soba (buckwheat) noodles
2 teaspoons sesame oil
2 spring onions (scallions), finely chopped
1 nori sheet, cut into matchstick-sized strips

Combine the rice vinegar, mirin, soy sauce and ginger in a small bowl. Set aside.

Bring a large saucepan of salted water to the boil. Blanch the spinach for about 20 seconds, then remove with a slotted spoon (reserve the water in the pan). Place the spinach in a bowl of ice-cold water for 30 seconds. Drain and squeeze out the moisture, then coarsely chop. Combine with the crabmeat and 2 tablespoons of the rice vinegar mixture.

Bring the pan of water back to the boil and cook the noodles for 5 minutes, or until just tender. Drain, then rinse under cold water. Toss with the sesame oil, spring onion and the remaining dressing. Divide the noodles among individual bowls, top with the spinach and crabmeat and scatter with nori.

SERVES 4

Prawn and vermicelli salad

Dressing
2 tablespoons dark soy sauce
1 tablespoon fish sauce
2 tablespoons lime juice
1 teaspoon grated lime zest
1 teaspoon caster (superfine)
    sugar
1 red chilli, seeded and finely
    chopped
2 teaspoons finely chopped
    fresh ginger

150 g (5½ oz) dried rice
    vermicelli
100 g (3½ oz) snow peas
    (mangetout), trimmed,
    halved widthways
3 tablespoons oil
100 g (3½ oz/⅔ cup) raw
    cashew nuts, chopped
24 raw prawns (shrimp), peeled
    and deveined, tails intact
1 large handful mint, chopped
1 large handful coriander
    (cilantro) leaves, chopped

To make the dressing, combine the ingredients in a small bowl.

Soak the vermicelli in boiling water for 5–7 minutes, or until soft. Drain and set aside. Blanch the snow peas in boiling salted water for 10 seconds. Drain and refresh under cold water.

Heat the oil in a wok and swirl to coat the side. When hot, add the cashews and stir-fry for 2–3 minutes, or until golden. Remove with a slotted spoon and drain on paper towels. Add the prawns to the wok and cook over high heat, stirring constantly, for 2–3 minutes, or until just pink. Transfer to a large bowl, pour on the dressing and toss. Chill.

Add the noodles, snow peas, mint, coriander and cashews, toss well and serve.

SERVES 4

Spicy lamb and noodle salad

1 tablespoon Chinese five-spice
3 tablespoons peanut oil
2 garlic cloves, crushed
2 lamb backstraps or loin fillets
   (about 250 g/9 oz each)
500 g (1 lb 2 oz) fresh shanghai
   (wheat) noodles
1½ teaspoons sesame oil
80 g (2¾ oz) snowpea
   (mangetout) sprouts
½ red capsicum (pepper), thinly
   sliced

4 spring onions (scallions),
   thinly sliced on the diagonal
2 tablespoons sesame seeds,
   toasted

Dressing
1 tablespoon finely chopped
   fresh ginger
1 tablespoon Chinese black
   vinegar
1 tablespoon Chinese rice wine
2 tablespoons peanut oil
2 teaspoons chilli oil

Combine the five-spice, 2 tablespoons of the peanut oil and garlic in a large bowl. Add the lamb and turn to coat well. Cover and marinate for 30 minutes.

Cook the noodles in a large saucepan of boiling water for 4–5 minutes. Drain, then rinse under cold water. Add the sesame oil and toss through.

Heat the remaining peanut oil in a large frying pan. Cook the lamb over medium–high heat for 3 minutes each side for medium–rare, or until cooked to your liking. Rest for 5 minutes, then thinly slice across the grain.

To make the dressing, combine the ingredients in a small bowl.

Place the noodles, lamb strips, snow pea sprouts, capsicum, spring onion and the dressing in a large bowl and toss gently. Sprinkle with the sesame seeds and serve.

SERVES 4

Eggplant and buckwheat noodle salad

10 g (¼ oz) dried shiitake
  mushrooms
350 g (12 oz) dried soba
  (buckwheat) noodles
2 teaspoons sesame oil
3 tablespoons tahini
1 tablespoon light soy sauce
1 tablespoon dark soy sauce
1 tablespoon honey
2 tablespoons lemon juice
3 tablespoons peanut oil

2 Japanese eggplants
  (aubergine), cut into very
  thin strips
2 carrots, julienned
10 spring onions (scallions),
  cut on the diagonal
6 fresh shiitake mushrooms,
  thinly sliced
50 g (1¾ oz) coriander
  (cilantro) leaves, roughly
  chopped

Soak the dried mushrooms in 125 ml (4 fl oz/½ cup) boiling water for 20 minutes. Drain, reserving the liquid. Discard the stems and thinly slice the caps.

Cook the noodles in a large saucepan of boiling water for 5 minutes, or until tender. Drain, then rinse under cold water. Toss with 1 teaspoon of the sesame oil.

Blend the tahini, both soy sauces, honey, lemon juice, 2 tablespoons of the reserved mushroom liquid and the remaining sesame oil in a food processor until smooth.

Heat 2 tablespoons of the peanut oil in a wok over high heat and swirl to coat the side. Add the eggplant and cook, turning often, for 4–5 minutes, or until soft and golden. Drain on crumpled paper towels. Heat the remaining peanut oil. Add the carrot, spring onion and fresh and dried mushrooms. Cook, stirring constantly, for 2 minutes, or until just softened. Remove from the heat and toss with the noodles, eggplant and dressing. Garnish with the coriander.

SERVES 4–6

Asian prawn and noodle salad

Dressing
2 tablespoons grated fresh ginger
2 tablespoons soy sauce
2 tablespoons sesame oil
4 tablespoons red wine vinegar
1 tablespoon sweet chilli sauce
2 garlic cloves, crushed
4 tablespoons kecap manis

250 g (9 oz) dried instant egg noodles
500 g (1 lb 2 oz) cooked large prawns (shrimp), peeled and
    deveined, tails intact
5 spring onions (scallions), sliced on the diagonal
2 tablespoons chopped coriander (cilantro) leaves
1 red capsicum (pepper), diced
100 g (3½ oz) snow peas (mangetout), halved
lime wedges, for serving

For the dressing, whisk together the fresh ginger, soy sauce, sesame oil, red wine vinegar, chilli sauce, garlic and kecap manis in a large bowl.

Cook the egg noodles in a large saucepan of boiling water for 2 minutes, or until tender, then drain thoroughly. Cool in a large bowl.

Add the dressing, prawns and remaining ingredients to the noodles and toss gently. Serve with lime wedges.

SERVES 4

Orange sweet potato and fried noodle salad

1.25 kg (2 lb 12 oz) orange
    sweet potato, peeled and cut
    into 2 cm (¾ inch) chunks
2 tablespoons oil
200 g (7 oz/1¼ cups) roasted
    unsalted cashew nuts
50 g (1¾ oz) coriander (cilantro)
    leaves, finely chopped
100 g (3½ oz) packet fried
    noodles

Dressing
¾ teaspoon red curry paste
90 ml (3 fl oz) coconut milk
2 tablespoons lime juice
1½ tablespoons soft brown
    sugar
2 tablespoons oil
4 garlic cloves, finely chopped
1 tablespoon finely chopped
    fresh ginger

Preheat the oven to 200°C (400°F/Gas 6). Place the sweet potato and oil in a bowl, and season lightly with salt and pepper. Toss together until well coated. Place on a baking tray and bake for 30 minutes, or until tender. Drain on crumpled paper towels.

To make the dressing, combine the curry paste, coconut milk, lime juice and sugar in a food processor.

Heat the oil in a small frying pan. Add the garlic and ginger and cook over low heat for 1–2 minutes, or until light brown. Remove and add to the dressing.

Place the sweet potato, cashews, coriander, dressing and the noodles in a large bowl and toss gently until combined. Serve immediately.

SERVES 4–6

NOTE: This is best assembled just before serving to prevent the noodles from becoming soggy.

stir-fry

Seared scallops with chilli bean paste

500 g (1 lb 2 oz) hokkien (egg)
    noodles
3 tablespoons peanut oil
20 scallops, without roe,
    membrane removed
1 large onion, cut into thin
    wedges
3 garlic cloves, crushed
1 tablespoon grated fresh ginger
1 tablespoon chilli bean paste
150 g (5½ oz) choy sum, cut
    into 5 cm (2 inch) lengths

3 tablespoons chicken stock
2 tablespoons light soy sauce
2 tablespoons kecap manis
1 large handful coriander
    (cilantro) leaves
90 g (3¼ oz/1 cup) bean sprouts
1 long red chilli, seeded and
    thinly sliced
1 teaspoon sesame oil
1 tablespoon Chinese rice wine

Soak the noodles in boiling water for 1 minute, or until tender and separated.
Drain, rinse under cold water, then drain again.

Heat a wok over high heat, add 2 tablespoons of the peanut oil and swirl to coat the
side. Add the scallops in batches and sear for 20 seconds each side, or until sealed.
Remove, then clean the wok. Add the remaining oil and swirl to coat. Stir-fry
the onion for 2 minutes, or until softened. Add the garlic and ginger and cook for
30 seconds. Stir in the chilli bean paste and cook for 1 minute, or until fragrant.

Add the choy sum to the wok with the noodles, stock, soy sauce and kecap manis.
Stir-fry for 2–3 minutes, or until the choy sum has wilted and the noodles have
absorbed most of the liquid. Return the scallops to the wok, add the coriander,
bean sprouts, chilli, sesame oil and rice wine, tossing gently until combined.

SERVES 4

Phad Thai

250 g (9 oz) dried flat rice noodles
1 small red chilli, chopped
2 garlic cloves, chopped
2 spring onions (scallions), sliced
1 tablespoon tamarind purée, combined with 1 tablespoon water
1½ tablespoons sugar
2 tablespoons fish sauce
2 tablespoons lime juice
2 tablespoons oil
2 eggs, beaten

150 g (5½ oz) pork fillet, thinly sliced
8 raw large prawns (shrimp), peeled and deveined, tails intact
100 g (3½ oz) fried tofu, julienned
90 g (3¼ oz/1 cup) bean sprouts
3 tablespoons chopped roasted peanuts
3 tablespoons coriander (cilantro) leaves
1 lime, cut into wedges

Soak the noodles in warm water for 10 minutes. Drain.

Pound the chilli, garlic and spring onion in a mortar and pestle. Gradually blend in the tamarind mixture, sugar, fish sauce and lime juice.

Heat a wok until very hot, add 1 tablespoon of the oil and swirl to coat the side. Add the egg, swirl to coat and cook for 1–2 minutes, or until set and cooked. Roll up, remove from the wok and thinly slice.

Heat the remaining oil, stir in the chilli mixture, and stir-fry for 30 seconds. Add the pork fillet and stir-fry for 2 minutes, or until tender. Add the prawns and stir-fry for 1 minute more. Stir in the noodles, egg, tofu and half the bean sprouts, and toss until heated through. Serve immediately, topped with the peanuts, coriander, lime and remaining bean sprouts.

SERVES 4–6

Pancit canton

1½ tablespoons oil
1 large onion, finely chopped
2 garlic cloves, finely chopped
2 x 2 cm (¾ x ¾ inch) piece
    fresh ginger, shredded
500 g (1 lb 2 oz) boneless,
    skinless chicken thighs,
    trimmed and cut into 2 cm
    (¾ inch) pieces
175 g (6 oz) Chinese cabbage
    (wong bok), shredded
1 carrot, julienned
200 g (7 oz) Chinese barbecued
    pork (char siu), cut into
    5 mm (¼ inch) thick pieces

3 teaspoons Chinese rice wine
2 teaspoons sugar
150 g (5½ oz) snow peas
    (mangetout), trimmed
375 ml (13 fl oz/1½ cups)
    chicken stock
1 tablespoon light soy sauce
225 g (8 oz) pancit canton (or
    Chinese e-fu) noodles (see
    Note page 182)
1 lemon, cut into wedges

Heat a wok over high heat, add the oil and swirl to coat the side. Add the onion and cook for 2 minutes, then add the garlic and ginger and cook for 1 minute. Add the chicken and cook for 2–3 minutes, or until browned. Stir in the cabbage, carrot, pork, rice wine and sugar and cook for a further 3–4 minutes, or until the pork is heated through and the vegetables are soft. Add the snow peas and cook for 1 minute. Remove the mixture from the wok.

Add the chicken stock and soy sauce to the wok and bring to the boil. Add the noodles and cook, stirring, for 3–4 minutes, or until soft and almost cooked through.

Return the stir-fry mixture to the wok and toss with the noodles for 1 minute, or until combined. Serve with lemon wedges.

SERVES 4

Fried noodles with chicken, pork and prawn

900 g (2 lb) fresh rice noodle
  rolls, at room temperature
100 ml (3½ fl oz) oil
2 garlic cloves, finely chopped
1 tablespoon grated fresh ginger
70 g (2½ oz) Chinese garlic
  chives, cut into 5 cm (2 inch)
  lengths
½ barbecued chicken, flesh cut
  into 1 cm (½ inch) slices
300 g (10½ oz) Chinese
  barbecued pork (char siu)
  fillet, cut into 1 cm (½ inch)
  slices

1 small red chilli, chopped
12 large cooked prawns
  (shrimp), peeled and
  deveined
180 g (6 oz/2 cups) bean sprouts
100 g (3½ oz) English spinach
2 eggs, beaten
2 teaspoons caster (superfine)
  sugar
125 ml (4 fl oz/½ cup) light soy
  sauce
2 tablespoons dark soy sauce
2 tablespoons fish sauce

Cut the noodle rolls lengthways into 2 cm (¾ inch) wide strips and gently separate.

Heat a wok over high heat, add 3 tablespoons of the oil and swirl to coat the side. Add the garlic and ginger and stir-fry for 30 seconds before adding the chives, chicken, pork, chilli and prawns. Stir-fry for 2 minutes, then add the bean sprouts and spinach, and cook for a further 1 minute.

Make a well in the centre of the mixture, add the egg and scramble for 1 minute, or until firm but not hard. Stir in the remaining oil, then stir in the noodles. Add the combined caster sugar, light and dark soy sauces, and fish sauce, and stir-fry for 2–3 minutes, or until heated through. Season with pepper.

SERVES 4

Spicy cellophane noodles with minced pork

200 g (7 oz) minced (ground) pork
1 teaspoon cornflour (cornstarch)
1½ tablespoons light soy sauce
2 tablespoons Chinese rice wine
1 teaspoon sesame oil
150 g (5½ oz) cellophane noodles (mung bean vermicelli)
2 tablespoons peanut oil

4 spring onions (scallions), finely chopped
1 garlic clove, crushed
1 tablespoon finely chopped fresh ginger
2 teaspoons chilli bean sauce
185 ml (6 fl oz/¾ cup) chicken stock
½ teaspoon sugar
2 spring onions (scallions), green part only, extra, thinly sliced on the diagonal

Combine the pork, cornflour, 1 tablespoon of the soy sauce, 1 tablespoon of the rice wine and ½ teaspoon of the sesame oil in a bowl, using a fork or your fingers. Cover with plastic wrap and marinate for 10–15 minutes.

Meanwhile, soak the noodles in boiling water for 3–4 minutes, or until soft. Drain, then rinse under cold water.

Heat a wok over high heat, add the peanut oil and swirl to coat the side. Cook the spring onion, garlic, ginger and chilli bean sauce for 10 seconds, then add the mince mixture and cook for 2 minutes, breaking up any lumps. Stir in the stock, sugar, ½ teaspoon salt and the remaining soy sauce, rice wine and sesame oil. Toss in the noodles. Bring to the boil, then reduce to a simmer, stirring occasionally, for about 7 minutes. Garnish with extra spring onion and serve.

SERVES 4

Stir-fried lamb with mint, chilli and shanghai noodles

400 g (14 oz) fresh shanghai (wheat) noodles
1 teaspoon sesame oil
2 tablespoons peanut oil
220 g (7¾ oz) lamb fillet, cut into thin strips
2 garlic cloves, crushed
2 red chillies, seeded and thinly sliced
1 tablespoon oyster sauce
2 teaspoons grated palm sugar (jaggery)
    or soft brown sugar
2 tablespoons fish sauce
2 tablespoons lime juice
1 large handful mint, chopped
lime wedges, to garnish

Cook the noodles in a large saucepan of boiling water for 4–5 minutes. Drain, then rinse under cold water. Add the sesame oil and toss through.

Heat the peanut oil in a wok over high heat and swirl to coat the side. Add the lamb and cook in batches for 1–2 minutes, or until just browned. Return all the meat to the wok and add the garlic and chilli. Cook for 30 seconds, then add the oyster sauce, palm sugar, fish sauce, lime juice and noodles. Cook for another 2–3 minutes, or until the noodles are warm. Stir in the mint and serve immediately with the lime wedges.

SERVES 4–6

Hokkien noodles with Asian greens and glazed tofu

300 g (10½ oz) firm tofu
3 tablespoons kecap manis
1 tablespoon mushroom soy
　sauce
1 tablespoon oyster sauce
450 g (1 lb) hokkien (egg)
　noodles
1 teaspoon sesame oil
1 tablespoon peanut oil

2 garlic cloves, crushed
1 tablespoon grated fresh ginger
1 onion, cut into wedges
450 g (1 lb) choy sum, roughly
　chopped
500 g (1 lb 2 oz) baby bok choy
　(pak choy), roughly chopped
2 tablespoons peanut oil, extra

Cut the tofu into 1 cm (½ inch) thick slices and place in a shallow, non-metallic dish. Mix together the kecap manis, soy and oyster sauces and pour over the tofu. Leave to marinate for about 15 minutes, then drain and reserve the marinade.

Soak the noodles in boiling water for 1 minute, or until tender and separated. Drain.

Heat the oils in a wok over medium heat and swirl to coat the side. Add the garlic, ginger and onion and stir-fry until the onion is soft. Remove from the wok. Add the green vegetables to the wok and stir-fry until just wilted. Remove. Add the noodles and the reserved marinade and stir-fry until heated through. Remove from the wok and divide among four plates.

Fry the tofu in the extra oil until it is browned on both sides. Serve the noodles topped with the tofu, green vegetables and onion mixture.

SERVES 4

Mud crab with rice noodles

1.5 kg (3 lb 5 oz) live mud crabs, each weighing approximately 250 g (9 oz)
150 g (5½ oz) dried thin rice noodles
5–6 tablespoons oil
2 red Asian shallots, thinly sliced
1 garlic clove, finely chopped
2 small red chillies, finely chopped

175 g (6 oz) bean sprouts, trimmed
175 g (6 oz) Chinese barbecued pork (char siu), cut into small pieces
3 tablespoons light soy sauce
2 tablespoons oyster sauce
2 tablespoons chopped coriander (cilantro) leaves

Freeze the crabs for 1 hour to immobilize them. Plunge them into boiling water for 2 minutes, then drain. Wash well with a stiff brush, then pat dry. Pull the apron back from underneath the crab and separate the shells. Remove the feathery gills and intestines. Twist off the claws. Using a cleaver or large knife, cut the crabs in half. Crack the claws using crab crackers or the back of a heavy knife.

Soak the noodles in boiling water for 10 minutes, then drain.

Heat a wok, add 2 tablespoons of the oil and, when just smoking, add half of the crab. Stir for 1 minute, reduce the heat to medium and cover with a lid. Cook for 6 minutes, or until the crab shells turn bright red. Lift onto a plate, then repeat, adding 1 tablespoon oil, if necessary. Remove the meat from the shells and claws.

Heat the rest of the oil in the wok, then stir-fry the shallots, garlic and chilli for 5 minutes. Add the bean sprouts and pork and cook for 2 minutes. Add the soy sauce, oyster sauce, noodles, crabmeat and coriander and stir until heated through.

SERVES 4

Mee grob

4 Chinese dried mushrooms
oil, for deep-frying
100 g (3½ oz) dried rice
   vermicelli
100 g (3½ oz) fried tofu, cut
   into matchsticks
4 garlic cloves, crushed
1 onion, chopped
1 boneless, skinless chicken
   breast, thinly sliced
6 spring onions (scallions),
   thinly sliced on the diagonal

8 green beans, sliced
8 raw prawns (shrimp), peeled
   and deveined, tails intact
4 tablespoons bean sprouts
coriander (cilantro) leaves, to
   garnish

Sauce
1 tablespoon soy sauce
3 tablespoons white vinegar
5 tablespoons sugar
3 tablespoons fish sauce
1 tablespoon sweet chilli sauce

Soak the mushrooms in boiling water for 20 minutes. Drain. Discard the stems and thinly slice the caps.

Fill a wok one-third full of oil and heat to 180°C (350°F), or until a cube of bread browns in 15 seconds. Cook the vermicelli in small batches until puffed and crispy. Drain on crumpled paper towel. Deep-fry the tofu in batches for 1 minute, or until crisp. Drain. Carefully remove all but 2 tablespoons of oil from the wok.

Reheat the wok until very hot. Add the garlic and onion and stir-fry for 1 minute. Add the chicken, mushrooms, half the spring onion and the beans. Stir-fry for 2 minutes, or until the chicken has almost cooked through. Add the prawns and stir-fry for a further 2 minutes, or until they just turn pink. Combine the sauce ingredients and add to the wok. Cook for 2 minutes until the meat and prawns are tender and the sauce is syrupy. Remove from the heat, and stir in the vermicelli, tofu, sprouts, coriander and remaining spring onion.

SERVES 4–6

Pork and brown bean noodles

3 tablespoons brown bean sauce
2 tablespoons hoisin sauce
185 ml (6 fl oz/¾ cup) chicken stock
½ teaspoon sugar
2 tablespoons oil
3 garlic cloves, finely chopped
6 spring onions (scallions), sliced, white and green parts separated
650 g (1 lb 7 oz) minced (ground) pork
500 g (1 lb 2 oz) fresh shanghai (wheat) noodles
1 telegraph (long) cucumber, halved lengthways,
    seeded and sliced on the diagonal
3 large handfuls coriander (cilantro) leaves
90 g (3¼ oz/1 cup) bean sprouts
1 tablespoon lime juice

Combine the brown bean and hoisin sauces, stock and sugar until smooth.

Heat the oil in a wok and swirl to coat the side. Add the garlic and the white part of the spring onion, and cook for 10–20 seconds. Add the pork and cook over high heat for 2–3 minutes, or until it has changed colour. Add the bean mixture, reduce the heat and simmer for 7–8 minutes.

Cook the noodles in a large saucepan of boiling water for 4–5 minutes. Drain, then rinse under cold water. Divide among serving bowls. Toss together the cucumber, coriander, bean sprouts, lime juice and remaining spring onion. Spoon the pork mixture over the noodles and top with the cucumber mixture.

SERVES 4–6

Beef and hokkien noodle stir-fry

350 g (12 oz) beef fillet, partially frozen
100 g (3½ oz) snow peas (mangetout)
600 g (1 lb 5 oz) hokkien (egg) noodles
2 tablespoons oil
1 large onion, cut into thin wedges
1 large carrot, thinly sliced on the diagonal
1 red capsicum (pepper), cut into thin strips
2 garlic cloves, crushed
1 teaspoon grated fresh ginger
200 g (7 oz) fresh shiitake mushrooms, sliced
3 tablespoons oyster sauce
2 tablespoons light soy sauce
1 tablespoon soft brown sugar
½ teaspoon Chinese five-spice

Cut the steak into thin slices. Top and tail the snow peas and slice in half diagonally. Soak the noodles in boiling water for 1 minute, or until tender and separated. Drain.

Heat 1 tablespoon of the oil in a wok and swirl to coat the side. Add the steak in batches and cook until brown. Remove from the wok and keep warm.

Heat the remaining oil in the wok and swirl to coat the side. When very hot, stir-fry the onion, carrot and capsicum for 2–3 minutes, or until tender. Add the garlic, ginger, snow peas and shiitake mushrooms, and cook for another minute before returning the steak to the wok.

Add to the wok, tossing well. Combine the oyster sauce with the soy sauce, brown sugar, five-spice and 1 tablespoon water and pour over the noodles. Toss until warmed through, then serve.

SERVES 4

Indonesian-style
fried noodles

400 g (14 oz) fresh flat egg
noodles (5 mm/¼ inch wide)
2 tablespoons oil
4 red Asian shallots, thinly sliced
2 garlic cloves, chopped
1 small red chilli, finely diced
200 g (7 oz) pork fillet, thinly
sliced across the grain
200 g (7 oz) boneless, skinless
chicken breast, thinly sliced
200 g (7 oz) small raw prawns
(shrimp), peeled and
deveined, tails intact
2 carrots, thinly sliced

2 Chinese cabbage (wong bok)
leaves, shredded
100 g (3½ oz) snake (yard-long)
beans, cut into 3 cm (1¼ inch)
lengths
3 tablespoons kecap manis
1 tablespoon light soy sauce
2 tomatoes, peeled, seeded and
chopped
4 spring onions (scallions), sliced
on the diagonal
1 tablespoon crisp fried onion
flakes

Cook the noodles in a large saucepan of boiling water for 1 minute, or until tender.
Drain, then rinse under cold water.

Heat a wok over high heat, add the oil and swirl to coat the side. Stir-fry the Asian
shallots for 30 seconds. Add the garlic, chilli and pork and stir-fry for 2 minutes, then
add the chicken and cook a further 2 minutes, or until the meat is golden and tender.

Add the prawns and stir-fry for another 2 minutes, or until pink. Stir in the carrot,
cabbage and beans and cook for 3 minutes, then add the noodles and gently stir-
fry for 4 minutes, or until heated through. Stir in the kecap manis, soy sauce,
chopped tomato and spring onion and stir-fry for 1–2 minutes. Season.

SERVES 4

Lamb with hokkien noodles and sour sauce

450 g (1 lb) hokkien (egg)
noodles
2 tablespoons oil
375 g (13 oz) lamb backstrap or
loin fillet, thinly sliced
against the grain
75 g (2½ oz) red Asian shallots,
thinly sliced
3 cloves garlic, crushed
2 teaspoons finely chopped
fresh ginger
1 small red chilli, seeded and
finely chopped

1½ tablespoons red curry paste
125 g (4½ oz) snow peas
(mangetout), trimmed and
halved on the diagonal
1 small carrot, julienned
125 ml (4 fl oz/½ cup) chicken
stock
1½ tablespoons grated palm
sugar (jaggery) or soft brown
sugar
1 tablespoon lime juice
small whole basil leaves, to
garnish

Cover the noodles with boiling water and soak for 1 minute. Drain and set aside.

Heat 1 tablespoon of the oil in a wok and swirl to coat the side. Stir-fry the lamb in batches over high heat for 2–3 minutes, or until it just changes colour. Remove from the wok and set aside.

Add the remaining oil, then the shallots, garlic, ginger and chilli and stir-fry for 1–2 minutes. Stir in the curry paste and cook for 1 minute. Add the snow peas, carrot and the lamb and combine. Cook over high heat, tossing often, for 1–2 minutes.

Add the stock, palm sugar and lime juice, toss to combine and cook for 2–3 minutes. Finally, add the noodles and cook for 1 minute, or until heated through. Divide among serving bowls and garnish with the basil.

SERVES 4–6

Chilli snake beans and noodles

325 g (11½ oz) fresh flat egg
    noodles (5 mm/¼ inch wide)
5 garlic cloves, peeled
3 red Asian shallots, chopped
1 small red chilli, seeded and
    chopped, plus extra, to
    garnish
3 coriander (cilantro) roots,
    chopped
2½ tablespoons oil

500 g (1 lb 2 oz) snake (yard-
    long) beans, cut into 4 cm
    (1½ inch) lengths
2½ tablespoons fish sauce
1½ tablespoons grated palm
    sugar (jaggery) or soft brown
    sugar
1 tablespoon kecap manis
1 tablespoon lime juice
1 tablespoon crisp fried onion
    flakes
lime wedges, to serve

Cook the noodles in a large saucepan of boiling water for 1 minute, or until tender. Drain well.

Place the garlic, red Asian shallots, chilli and coriander roots in a mortar and pestle or small food processor and grind to a smooth paste — add a little water if necessary.

Heat a wok over high heat, add the oil and swirl to coat the side. Stir in the paste and cook for 1 minute, or until fragrant. Add the beans, stir-fry for 2 minutes, then reduce the heat to low, cover and steam for 2 minutes. Increase the heat to high, add the fish sauce, palm sugar and kecap manis and stir-fry for 1 minute. Toss the noodles through the bean mixture for 1–2 minutes, or until heated through. Drizzle with the lime juice. Divide among serving bowls. Garnish with the crisp fried onion flakes and sliced chilli and serve with lime wedges.

SERVES 4

Vegetarian phad Thai

400 g (14 oz) dried flat rice
    noodle sticks
2 tablespoons oil
2 eggs, lightly beaten
1 onion, cut into thin wedges
2 garlic cloves, crushed
1 small red capsicum (pepper),
    cut into thin strips
100 g (3½ oz) fried tofu, cut
    into 5 mm (¼ inch) wide
    strips

6 spring onions (scallions),
    thinly sliced on the diagonal
2 large handfuls coriander
    (cilantro) leaves, chopped
3 tablespoons soy sauce
2 tablespoons lime juice
1 tablespoon soft brown sugar
2 teaspoons sambal oelek
90 g (3¼ oz/1 cup) bean shoots
3 tablespoons chopped roasted
    unsalted peanuts

Cook the noodles in a saucepan of boiling water for 5–10 minutes, or until tender.
Drain and set aside.

Heat a wok until very hot, add 1 tablespoon of the oil and swirl to coat the side. Add
the egg, swirl to coat and cook for 1–2 minutes, or until set and cooked. Roll up,
remove from the wok and thinly slice.

Heat the remaining oil in the wok. Cook the onion, garlic and capsicum over high
heat for 2–3 minutes, or until the onion has softened. Add the noodles, tossing
well. Stir in the omelette strips, tofu, spring onion and half the coriander.

Pour in the combined soy sauce, lime juice, sugar and sambal oelek, then toss to
coat the noodles. Sprinkle the bean shoots over the top and garnish with the peanuts
and the remaining coriander. Serve immediately.

SERVES 4

Noodles with beef

500 g (1 lb 2 oz) fresh rice
noodle roll, at room
temperature
2 tablespoons oil
2 eggs, lightly beaten
500 g (1 lb 2 oz) rump steak,
thinly sliced
3 tablespoons kecap manis

1½ tablespoons soy sauce
1½ tablespoons fish sauce
300 g (10½ oz) Chinese broccoli
(gai larn), cut into 5 cm
(2 inch) lengths
¼ teaspoon white pepper
lemon wedges, to serve

Cut the noodle roll lengthways into 2 cm (¾ inch) wide strips. Gently separate the strips — run under cold water if necessary.

Heat a wok until hot, add 1 tablespoon of the oil and swirl to coat the side. Add the egg, swirl to coat and cook for 1–2 minutes, or until set and cooked. Roll up, remove from the wok and thinly slice.

Reheat the wok over high heat, add the remaining oil and swirl to coat. Cook the beef in batches for 3 minutes, or until brown. Remove.

Reduce the heat to medium, add the noodles and cook for 2 minutes. Combine the kecap manis, soy and fish sauces. Add to the wok with the broccoli and white pepper, then stir-fry for 2 minutes. Return the egg and beef to the wok and cook for 3 minutes, or until the broccoli has wilted and the noodles are soft but not breaking. Serve with the lemon.

SERVES 4–6

Teriyaki beef with greens and crispy noodles

450 g (1 lb) sirloin steak, cut
   into thin strips
125 ml (4 fl oz/½ cup) teriyaki
   marinade
oil, for deep-frying
100 g (3½ oz) dried rice
   vermicelli
2 tablespoons peanut oil

1 onion, sliced
3 garlic cloves, crushed
1 red chilli, seeded and finely
   chopped
200 g (7 oz) carrots, julienned
600 g (1 lb 5 oz) choy sum, cut
   into 3 cm (1¼ inch) lengths
1 tablespoon lime juice

Combine the beef and teriyaki marinade in a non-metallic bowl, cover with plastic wrap and marinate for 2 hours.

Fill a wok one-third full of oil and heat to 190°C (375°F), or until a cube of bread browns in 10 seconds. Separate the vermicelli noodles into small bundles and deep-fry until they sizzle and puff up. Drain on crumpled paper towels. Drain the oil and carefully pour it into a heatproof bowl to cool before discarding.

Heat 1 tablespoon of the peanut oil in the wok. When the oil is nearly smoking, add the beef (reserving the marinade) and cook in batches over high heat for 1–2 minutes. Remove to a plate. Heat the remaining oil. Add the onion and stir-fry for 3–4 minutes. Add the garlic and chilli and cook for 30 seconds. Add the carrot and choy sum and stir-fry for 3–4 minutes, or until tender.

Return the beef to the wok with the lime juice and reserved marinade and cook over high heat for 3 minutes. Add the noodles, toss well briefly, and serve immediately.

SERVES 4

Ginger chicken stir-fry with hokkien noodles

2½ tablespoons finely shredded
    fresh ginger
3 tablespoons mirin
2 tablespoons soy sauce
600 g (1 lb 5 oz) chicken
    tenderloins or boneless,
    skinless chicken breasts, cut
    diagonally into thin strips

180 g (6 oz) fresh baby corn
350 g (12 oz) choy sum
150 g (5½ oz) fresh oyster
    mushrooms
500 g (1 lb 2 oz) hokkien (egg)
    noodles
2 tablespoons oil
2 tablespoons oyster sauce

Combine the ginger, mirin and soy sauce in a non-metallic bowl. Add the chicken, coat well, then marinate while preparing the vegetables.

Cut the corn in half lengthways; trim the ends off the choy sum and cut into 6 cm (2½ inch) lengths. If the mushrooms are very large, cut them in half. Soak the noodles in boiling water for 1 minute, or until tender and separated. Drain and refresh under cold running water.

Heat a wok until very hot, add 1 tablespoon of the oil and swirl to coat the side. Remove the chicken from the marinade with a slotted spoon (reserving the marinade) and cook in two batches over very high heat for 2 minutes, or until brown and just cooked. Remove from the wok.

Add the remaining oil to the wok and stir-fry the mushrooms and corn for 1–2 minutes, or until just softened. Add the remaining marinade, bring to the boil, then add the chicken, choy sum and noodles. Stir in the oyster sauce and cook, tossing well, for 1–2 minutes, or until the choy sum has wilted slightly and the noodles are warmed through.

SERVES 4

Ma po tofu with noodles

450 g (1 lb) silken firm tofu, cut into 2 cm (¾ inch) cubes
375 g (13 oz) hokkien (egg) noodles
2 teaspoons cornflour (cornstarch)
1 tablespoon peanut oil
2 teaspoons finely chopped fresh ginger
2 spring onions (scallions), thinly sliced on the diagonal
225 g (8 oz) minced (ground) pork

1½ tablespoons salted black beans, rinsed and roughly chopped
1 tablespoon chilli bean paste
1 tablespoon dark soy sauce
125 ml (4 fl oz/½ cup) chicken stock
1 tablespoon Chinese rice wine
2 garlic cloves, finely chopped
ground white pepper, to taste
2 spring onions (scallions), green part only, extra, thinly sliced on the diagonal
½ teaspoon sesame oil

Place the tofu on paper towels to drain the excess moisture.

Soak the noodles in boiling water for 1 minute, or until tender and separated. Drain well, rinse under cold water and drain again. Divide among four serving bowls. Combine the cornflour and 1 tablespoon water in a small bowl.

Heat the peanut oil in a wok over high heat and swirl to coat the side. Add the ginger and spring onion and cook for 30 seconds, then add the pork and stir-fry for 2 minutes, or until almost cooked. Add the black beans, chilli bean paste and soy sauce and stir-fry for 1 minute. Stir in the stock, rice wine and tofu and heat through.

Stir the cornflour mixture and garlic into the wok and cook for a further minute, or until thickened. Spoon over the noodles and season with ground white pepper. Garnish with the extra spring onion and drizzle with the sesame oil.

SERVES 4

Yaki udon

5 dried shiitake mushrooms
2 garlic cloves, crushed
2 teaspoons grated fresh ginger
125 ml (4 fl oz/½ cup) Japanese
   soy sauce
2 tablespoons rice vinegar
2 tablespoons sugar
1 tablespoon lemon juice
500 g (1 lb 2 oz) fresh udon
   noodles
2 tablespoons peanut oil

500 g (1 lb 2 oz) boneless,
   skinless chicken thighs, sliced
1 small red capsicum (pepper),
   thinly sliced
150 g (5½ oz/2 cups) shredded
   cabbage
4 spring onions (scallions),
   thinly sliced
1 tablespoon sesame oil
white pepper, to taste
2 tablespoons drained shredded
   pickled ginger

Soak the mushrooms in boiling water for 10 minutes. Drain, reserving 3 tablespoons of the liquid. Discard the stems, squeeze the caps dry and thinly slice.

Combine half the garlic with the ginger, soy sauce, vinegar, sugar, lemon juice and reserved soaking liquid.

Soak the noodles in boiling water for 2 minutes, or until tender. Drain.

Heat a wok over high heat, add half the peanut oil and swirl to coat the side. Add the chicken in batches and stir-fry for 5 minutes, or until browned. Remove from the wok. Add the remaining peanut oil and swirl to coat. Add the remaining garlic, mushrooms, capsicum and cabbage, and stir-fry for 2–3 minutes, or until softened. Add the noodles and stir-fry for another minute. Return the chicken to the wok and add the spring onion, sesame oil and soy sauce mixture, stirring until well combined and heated through. Season generously with white pepper and scatter with the pickled ginger.

SERVES 4

Mushroom long-life noodles

400 g (14 oz) pancit canton (or Chinese e-fu) noodles (see Note)
1 tablespoon peanut oil
3 tablespoons soy sauce
1½ tablespoons mushroom soy sauce
1 teaspoon sesame oil
1 teaspoon sugar
250 ml (9 fl oz/1 cup) vegetable stock
1 tablespoon grated fresh ginger
2 garlic cloves, crushed
250 g (9 oz) fresh shiitake mushrooms, sliced
250 g (9 oz) shimeji mushrooms, separated
125 g (4½ oz) dried black fungus (wood ears), sliced
250 g (9 oz) enoki mushrooms, ends trimmed
30 g (1 oz) spring onions (scallions), thinly sliced on the diagonal

Cook the noodles in a large saucepan of boiling water for 3 minutes. Drain, then rinse under cold water. Toss the noodles with 1 teaspoon of the peanut oil.

Mix together the soy sauce, mushroom soy sauce, sesame oil, sugar and vegetable stock in a small bowl.

Heat the remaining peanut oil in a wok over high heat and swirl to coat the side. Add the ginger and garlic and stir-fry for 1 minute. Add the shiitake mushrooms, shimeji mushrooms and dried black fungus and stir-fry for 3 minutes. Add the noodles, enoki mushrooms, spring onion and combined sauce ingredients. Gently toss, cooking until the noodles have absorbed the sauce.

SERVES 4

NOTE: Pancit canton noodles are round cakes of pre-boiled, deep-fried noodles; be careful because they break easily. They are available in Asian grocery stores.

Udon noodle stir-fry with miso dressing

1 tablespoon white miso
1 tablespoon Japanese soy sauce
2 tablespoons sake
1/2 teaspoon sugar
400 g (14 oz) fresh udon noodles
1 tablespoon oil
5 spring onions (scallions), cut into 5 cm (2 inch) lengths
1 red capsicum (pepper), thinly sliced
100 g (3 1/2 oz) fresh shiitake mushrooms, sliced
150 g (5 1/2 oz) snow peas (mangetout), sliced lengthways into strips

Combine the miso with the soy sauce to form a smooth paste. Add the sake and sugar and mix well.

Cook the noodles in a saucepan of boiling water for 1–2 minutes, or until tender. Drain, then rinse under cold water.

Heat the oil in a wok over high heat and swirl to coat the side. Add the spring onion and capsicum and toss frequently for 1–2 minutes, or until softened slightly. Add the mushrooms and snow peas and stir-fry for 2–3 minutes, or until tender.

Add the noodles and miso mixture to the wok and toss until well combined. Serve immediately.

SERVES 4

Sweet ginger and chilli vegetables with rice noodles

500 g (1 lb 2 oz) fresh rice
noodle roll, at room
temperature (see Note)
2 tablespoons peanut oil
1 teaspoon sesame oil
3 tablespoons grated fresh
ginger
1 onion, thinly sliced
1 red capsicum (pepper), sliced
100 g (3½ oz) fresh shiitake
mushrooms, sliced

200 g (7 oz) baby corn, halved
500 g (1 lb 2 oz) Chinese
broccoli (gai larn), sliced
200 g (7 oz) snowpeas
(mangetout)
3 tablespoons sweet chilli sauce
2 tablespoons light soy sauce
2 tablespoons dark soy sauce
1 tablespoon lime juice
16 Thai basil leaves

Cut the noodle roll lengthways into 2 cm (¾ inch) wide strips, then cut each strip into three lengths. Gently separate the strips — run under cold water if necessary.

Heat the oils in a wok and swirl to coat the side. Add the ginger and onion and stir-fry until the onion is soft. Add the vegetables and stir-fry until brightly coloured and just tender.

Add the noodles to the vegetables and stir-fry until the noodles start to soften. Stir in the combined sauces and lime juice and cook until heated through. Remove from the heat, toss through the basil leaves and serve.

SERVES 4

NOTE: Rice noodle rolls should not be refrigerated, as they are very difficult to separate when cold.

Singapore noodles

375 g (13 oz) fresh thin egg
noodles
10 g (¼ oz) dried Chinese
mushrooms
2½ teaspoons sugar
1½ tablespoons soy sauce
2 tablespoons Chinese rice wine
1½ tablespoons Indian madras
curry powder
150 ml (5 fl oz) coconut milk
125 ml (4 fl oz/½ cup) chicken
stock
2 eggs
1 tablespoon sesame oil
3 tablespoons peanut oil

2 garlic cloves, finely chopped
1 tablespoon finely chopped
fresh ginger
2 small red chillies, seeded and
finely chopped
3 spring onions (scallions), sliced
300 g (10½ oz) small raw
prawns (shrimp), peeled,
deveined and halved
150 g (5½ oz) Chinese
barbecued pork (char siu),
thinly sliced
115 g (4 oz/¾ cup) frozen peas
coriander (cilantro) leaves, to
garnish

Cook the noodles in a large saucepan of boiling water for 1 minute. Drain, then
rinse under cold water.

Soak the mushrooms in a bowl with 125 ml (4 fl oz/½ cup) hot water for 10 minutes.
Drain and reserve the liquid, then discard the hard stalks and thinly slice the caps.
Combine the reserved liquid with the sugar, soy sauce, rice wine, curry powder,
coconut milk and stock. Lightly beat the eggs and sesame oil together.

Heat 2 tablespoons of the peanut oil in a wok and swirl to coat the side. Cook the
garlic, ginger, chilli and mushrooms for 30 seconds. Add the spring onion, prawns,
pork, peas and noodles. Stir in the mushroom liquid mixture. Add the egg mixture
in a thin stream and toss until warmed through. Serve garnished with coriander.

SERVES 4

Seafood noodles

6 dried shiitake mushrooms
400 g (14 oz) fresh thick egg
noodles
1 egg white, lightly beaten
3 teaspoons cornflour
(cornstarch)
1 teaspoon crushed sichuan
peppercorns
250 g (9 oz) firm white fish, cut
into 2 cm (¾ inch) cubes
200 g (7 oz) raw prawns
(shrimp), peeled and
deveined, tails intact

3 tablespoons oil
3 spring onions (scallions), sliced
on the diagonal
2 garlic cloves, crushed
1 tablespoon grated fresh
ginger
225 g (8 oz) tin bamboo shoots,
thinly sliced
2 tablespoons hot chilli sauce
1 tablespoon soy sauce
2 tablespoons Chinese rice wine
185 ml (6 fl oz/¾ cup) fish stock

Soak the mushrooms in 125 ml (4 fl oz/½ cup) warm water for 20 minutes. Drain. Discard the stems, then thinly slice the caps.

Cook the noodles in a saucepan of boiling water for 2–3 minutes, or until just tender. Drain.

Blend the egg white, cornflour and half the peppercorns to a smooth paste. Dip the seafood into the mixture. Heat 2 tablespoons of the oil in a wok. Drain the excess batter from the seafood and stir-fry in batches over high heat until crisp and golden. Drain on paper towels.

Clean the wok and heat the remaining oil. Toss the spring onion, garlic, ginger, bamboo shoots, mushrooms, and remaining pepper over high heat for 1 minute. Stir in the chilli sauce, soy sauce, rice wine, fish stock and noodles. Add the seafood and toss until heated through.

SERVES 4

Rice noodles with beef, black beans and capsicum

300 g (10½ oz) rump steak
1 garlic clove, crushed
3 tablespoons oyster sauce
2 teaspoons sugar
2 tablespoons soy sauce
5 tablespoons black bean sauce
2 teaspoons cornflour
   (cornstarch)
¾ teaspoon sesame oil

1.25 kg (2 lb 12 oz) fresh or
   600 g (1 lb 5 oz) dried flat
   rice noodles
1½ tablespoons peanut oil
2 red capsicums (peppers), sliced
1 green capsicum (pepper),
   sliced
1 handful coriander (cilantro)
   leaves

Cut the steak across the grain into thin slices and put it in a bowl with the garlic, oyster sauce, sugar, soy sauce, black bean sauce, cornflour and sesame oil. Mix everything together, making sure all the slices are well coated.

If you are using dried rice noodles, soak them in boiling water for 10 minutes, or until they are opaque and soft. If your noodles are particularly dry, they may need a little longer. Drain the noodles.

Heat the peanut oil in a wok and swirl to coat the side. Add the capsicum and stir-fry for 1–2 minutes until it is starting to soften, then add the meat mixture and cook for 1 minute. Add the noodles and toss everything together well. Keep cooking until the meat is cooked through and everything is hot, then toss in the coriander leaves and stir once before turning off the heat. Serve straight away.

SERVES 4

Japanese pork and noodle stir-fry

350 g (12 oz) pork fillet
4 tablespoons soy sauce
3 tablespoons mirin
2 teaspoons grated fresh ginger
2 garlic cloves, crushed
1½ tablespoons soft brown
    sugar
500 g (1 lb 2 oz) hokkien (egg)
    noodles
2 tablespoons oil

1 onion, cut into thin wedges
1 red capsicum (pepper), cut
    into thin strips
2 carrots, thinly sliced on the
    diagonal
4 spring onions (scallions),
    thinly sliced on the diagonal
200 g (7 oz) fresh shiitake
    mushrooms, sliced

Trim the pork of any excess fat or sinew and slice thinly. Combine the soy sauce, mirin, ginger, garlic and sugar in a large non-metallic bowl, add the pork and toss to coat. Cover with plastic wrap and refrigerate for 10 minutes.

Meanwhile, soak the noodles in boiling water for 1 minute, or until tender and separated. Drain.

Heat a large wok over high heat, add 1 tablespoon of the oil and swirl to coat the side. Drain the pork, reserving the marinade, and stir-fry in batches for 3 minutes, or until browned. Remove and keep warm.

Reheat the wok over high heat, add the remaining oil and swirl to coat. Add the onion, capsicum and carrot, and stir-fry for 2–3 minutes, or until just tender, then add the spring onion and shiitake mushroom. Cook for another 2 minutes, then return the pork to the wok. Add the noodles to the wok with the reserved marinade. Toss to combine and cook for another 1 minute, or until heated through, then serve.

SERVES 4

index

First published in 2009 by Murdoch Books Pty Limited

Murdoch Books Australia
Pier 8/9, 23 Hickson Road
Millers Point NSW 2000
Phone: +61 (0) 2 8220 2000
Fax: +61 (0) 2 8220 2558
www.murdochbooks.com.au

Murdoch Books UK Limited
Erico House, 6th Floor
93–99 Upper Richmond Road
Putney, London SW15 2TG
Phone: +44 (0) 20 8785 5995
Fax: +44 (0) 20 8785 5985
www.murdochbooks.co.uk

Chief Executive: Juliet Rogers
Publishing Director: Kay Scarlett

Design manager: Vivien Valk
Project manager: Gordana Trifunovic
Editor: Zoë Harpham
Design concept: Alex Frampton
Designer: Susanne Geppert
Production: Kita George
Recipes developed by the Murdoch Books Test Kitchen

Printed by Sing Cheong Printing Co. Ltd in 2009. PRINTED IN HONG KONG.

ISBN 978 1 74196 376 2 (pbk).

A catalogue record for this book is available from the British Library.

IMPORTANT: Those who might be at risk from the effects of salmonella poisoning (the elderly, pregnant women, young children and those suffering from immune deficiency diseases) should consult their doctor with any concerns about eating raw eggs.

CONVERSION GUIDE: You may find cooking times vary depending on the oven you are using. For fan-forced ovens, as a general rule, set the oven temperature to 20°C (35°F) lower than indicated in the recipe. We have used 20 ml (4 teaspoon) tablespoon measures. If you are using a 15 ml (3 teaspoon) tablespoon, for most recipes the difference will not be noticeable. However, for recipes using baking powder, gelatine, bicarbonate of soda (baking soda), small amounts of flour and cornflour (cornstarch), add an extra teaspoon for each tablespoon specified.